Anne Hürtgen

Sprachmittlung

Englisch

Klasse 9–10

Die Autorin

Dr. Anne Hürtgen ist Lehrerin für Englisch, Französisch und Deutsch als Zweitsprache. Nach ihrer Promotion zum Thema Zweitspracherwerb war sie mehrere Jahre als Gymnasiallehrerin und in der Ausbildung von Lehramtsstudenten tätig; seit 2016 ist sie Studienrätin an einer Gesamtschule bei Frankfurt am Main.
Ihr Schwerpunkt ist die Förderung der Mündlichkeit und der interkulturellen Kommunikationskompetenz im Fremdsprachenunterricht.

Projektleitung: Gabriele Teubner-Nicolai, Berlin
Redaktion: Anke Kellerhoff, Wilnsdorf
Umschlagkonzeption/-gestaltung: Corinna Babylon, Berlin
Umschlagbild: Shutterstock / Greens87
Layout / technische Umsetzung: LemmeDESIGN, Berlin

www.cornelsen.de

1. Auflage 2018

© 2018 Cornelsen Verlag GmbH, Berlin

Druck: H. Heenemann, Berlin

ISBN 978-3-589-15344-2

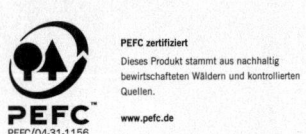

PEFC zertifiziert
Dieses Produkt stammt aus nachhaltig bewirtschafteten Wäldern und kontrollierten Quellen.
PEFC
www.pefc.de
PEFC/04-31-1156

Inhaltsverzeichnis

Vorwort

Sprachmittlung ermöglicht die Verständigung zwischen Menschen, die unterschiedliche Sprachen sprechen und sich deshalb nicht direkt verstehen können. Dabei geht es nicht um eine wortwörtliche Übersetzung, sondern um die Übertragung der in der jeweiligen Situation relevanten Informationen.

Sprachmittlung kann im Alltag in verschiedenen mündlichen und schriftlichen Situationen erforderlich werden. Je nach Situation wird Sprachmittlung aus dem Deutschen ins Englische, aus dem Englischen ins Deutsche oder zwischen noch mehr Sprachen benötigt.
Demensprechend ist die Sprachmittlung eine wichtige kommunikative Kompetenz, die auch im Englischunterricht häufig geübt und in mündlichen und schriftlichen Klassenarbeiten und Abschlussprüfungen abgefragt wird.

Dieses Übungsheft hat das Ziel, Schülerinnen und Schüler systematisch auf schriftliche und mündliche Formen der Sprachmittlung in realistischen Situationen vorzubereiten und die entsprechenden Sprachmittlungsfähigkeiten zu vermitteln:
- Verstehen des Ausgangstextes bzw. der Ausgangssituation,
- Berücksichtigung des/der Adressaten und der Kommunikationssituation,
- Zusammenfassen der wesentlichen Punkte,
- Ausdrücken der relevanten Informationen in eigenen Worten.

Die Übungen in diesem Heft bieten vielfältige realistische Anwendungssituationen zum Üben im Unterricht und zu Hause. Mittels Lese- und Hörtexten zu verschiedenen lebensweltnahen und altersangemessenen Themen werden neben der Sprachmittlungskompetenz auch die Lese- und Hörverstehenskompetenz, sprachliche Kompetenzen und das landeskundliche Wissen erweitert.

Im ersten Teil können die Schülerinnen und Schüler ihre Sprachmittlungsfähigkeit testen und aufgrund dessen entscheiden, welche Teilkompetenzen sie weiter verbessern möchten. Dafür bietet der zweite Teil systematische Übungen und authentische Sprachmittlungsaufgaben mit schrittweiser Anleitung. Die Beispielprüfungen im dritten Teil ermöglichen eine gezielte Klassenarbeits- und Prüfungsvorbereitung. Im vierten Teil finden sich zur Selbstüberprüfung die Lösungen zu allen Übungen sowie Transkripte zu den Hörübungen. Die Höraufgaben befinden sich auf der CD.

Viel Spaß und Erfolg bei der Arbeit mit diesem Übungsheft und der Sprachmittlung im Englischunterricht wünscht Ihnen und euch

Dr. Anne Hürtgen

Check your mediation skills

In this section you have the chance to check your mediation skills. There are four different tasks, based on various kinds of reading and listening materials. The first task requires mediation from English to German, the second and third from German to English and the last task in both directions. After each task you can compare your solutions to the model solutions in chapter 4 (p. 50 ff.) and evaluate yourself with the help of a self-evaluation grid.

A   English language vacation
(Mediation: English → German)

SITUATION

You would like to take a Junior Vacation course in Brighton during the next spring holidays, but you are afraid that your parents might be against the idea. In order to convince them, you want to tell them about the language course.

DOCUMENT

JUNIOR VACATION

Junior Vacation courses provide full education, activity, social and event programmes for students from all over the world. Junior Vacation courses combine British hospitality in a carefully selected homestay with a full programme of study and activity. There are winter, spring and summer courses at the college, and in summer BLC uses the facilities of the University of Brighton, Grand Parade and Circus Street. All teenage courses run 7 nights Sunday to Sunday for arrivals and departures.

Junior Vacation	Brighton Spring 2018
Lessons per Week	20 (15 hours)
Daily Schedule	09:00 – 12:30 + activities
Class Size	13 (16 max)
Course Book	Included
Course Code	S20
Course Dates	18. 03. 18 – 08. 04. 18
English Levels	Elementary +
Course Length	1 to 3 weeks
Age Range	12 – 7
Half-day Activities	Every day
Evening Activities	3/week
Excursions	1 full day & 1 half day/week
Cost	410 GBP/week

● You study in an international group and enjoy 4 half-day activities, 3 evenings and 1 half-day and 1 full-day excursion every week.
● BLC provides freshly-made packed lunches every day.
● BLC is open over the Easter weekend, classes and activities as usual.

Quelle: http://www.brightonic.co.uk/junior-vacation/ (zuletzt aufgerufen am 15. 01. 2018)
Foto: Fotolia / dglimages

TASKS

1. Prepare your answers (in German) to some questions your parents are probably going to ask you:

Dauer und Kosten der Sprachkurse?

Welche Leistungen sind im Preis eingeschlossen?

Weitere Vorteile der Junior Vacation am Brighton Language College?

2. Compare your answers to the solution on p. 50 and fill in the following table.

Criteria	Evaluation of your mediation text: ☺☺☹	Comments
I included all the important information.		
I did not include any irrelevant information / too many details.		
I could understand the relevant information and express it in the other language.		
I considered the context, addressee(s) and purpose of the mediation task.		

B Spaß im Stau
(Mediation: German → English)

SITUATION

Jamie, your exchange partner from Scotland, has just written you an email. In this email he tells you that he is going on holiday with his parents and that he is not looking forward to the long car ride. Since you have just discovered a newspaper article about games to play in the car, you want to suggest these games to Jamie.

DOCUMENT

Kindertipp   16. Juni 2017, 19:04 Uhr

SPASS IM STAU

Jeder kennt sich irgendwo besonders gut aus. In der Rubrik „Kindertipp" verraten Leser ihre Tricks im Alltag. Diesmal erzählt Henriette, 9, wie man sich auf nicht enden wollenden Autofahrten die Zeit vertreiben kann.

Reiseziel-ABC

Zu jedem Buchstaben des Alphabets muss man etwas finden, was zu dem Ort passt, wo man in den Urlaub hinfährt – oder gerade herkommt. Also für Rom zum Beispiel: A wie allerbestes Wetter, B wie Bahnhof, C wie Caesar, D wie durstig und so weiter. Das ist gar nicht so einfach. Mit dem, was gilt, kann man deswegen großzügig sein. […]

Kennzeichen-Sätze

Autokennzeichen kann man gut verwenden, um Sätze zu erfinden. Aus BN-NH wird dann zum Beispiel: „Beste Nudeln nur hier!".

Weiterreden

Einer fängt an und sagt ein Wort, das aus zwei Teilen besteht, zum Beispiel „Sonnenbrille". Der Nächste muss dann ein Wort finden mit dem letzten Teil als erstes, also etwa „Brillenglas". Es geht weiter, zum Beispiel mit „Glashaus". […]

Kettengeschichte

Jede Geschichte beginnt mit einem Satz. Zum Beispiel: „Es war einmal ein Mädchen." Dann ist der Nächste dran mit dem zweiten Satz. Das geht immer weiter, bis euch nichts mehr einfällt oder ihr angekommen seid.

Quelle: http://www.sueddeutsche.de/leben/kindertipp-spass-im-stau-1.3544906 (zuletzt aufgerufen am 15.01.2018)
Foto: Fotolia / detailblick-foto

TASKS

1. Read the newspaper article and write an email to your exchange partner Jamie (in English), in which you explain the games to him. You can start as follows:

Von:

An: Jamie

Dear Jamie,

Thanks for your email, I was happy to hear from you!

It is really great that you are going on holidays so soon, but the car trip sounds really long and boring. You know I might have some (German) games you could play with your sister or your parents while in the car:

Please let me know whether you liked the games. Have a great journey!

Best wishes,

Your friend

2. Compare your email to the solution on p. 50 and fill in the following table.

Criteria	Evaluation of your mediation text: ☺ ☺ ☹	Comments
I included all the important information.		
I did not include any irrelevant information / too many details.		
I could understand the relevant information and express it in the other language.		
I considered the context, addressee(s) and purpose of the mediation task.		
I used paragraphs and linking words to structure my email.		

C Berlin – Hauptstadt am Wasser
(Mediation: German → English)

SITUATION

Your Irish exchange partner Susan has to do a presentation for her geography class on the following documentary on Berlin. Since her German is not very good, she has difficulty understanding it.

DOCUMENT

"Berlin – Hauptstadt am Wasser", Deutsche Welle, 24. 05. 2017 (3:05 min., see CD / Track 1)

Foto: Fotolia / Katja Xenikis

TASKS

1. Write an email to your exchange partner Susan in which you summarize the documentary in English. You can start as follows:

Von: me
An: Susan

Dear Susan,

Thanks for your email, I was happy to hear from you!

The documentary on Berlin and its water-related attractions was really interesting. I found the following key points for your presentation:

General information on Berlin's waterways:

Information on Wannsee and Strandbad Wannsee:

Information on the boat tour from Wannsee to Museumsinsel:

If you have any more questions, please let me know. I hope I have been able to help you with your presentation!
Best wishes,
Your friend

2. Compare your email to the solution on p. 50 and fill in the following table.

Criteria	Evaluation of your mediation text: ☺ ☺ ☹	Comments
I included all the important information.		
I did not include any irrelevant information / too many details.		
I could understand the relevant information and express it in the other language.		
I considered the context, addressee(s) and purpose of the mediation task.		

D The new exchange student (Mediation: English ↔ German)

SITUATION

Brian from London is a new exchange student in your class. Your teacher, Frau Meyer, asks you to help Brian and to show him his way around at your school. Unfortunately, Frau Meyer's English is not very good, and Brian does not speak much German yet.

TASKS

1. Mediate from German to English for Frau Meyer and from English to German for Brian.

Frau Meyer: Kannst du Brian bitte sagen, dass die Schule jeden Tag um 8 Uhr beginnt? Morgen hat er in der ersten Stunde Chemie. Er soll also bitte direkt zum Chemieraum gehen.

Du (auf Englisch zu Brian):

Brian: Yes, thanks, I will try, but where is the chemistry lab? And do I need any books or lab equipment?

Du (auf Deutsch zu Frau Meyer):

Frau Meyer: Der Chemieraum ist am anderen Ende der Schule, direkt links vom Haupteingang aus. Vielleicht könnt ihr beide euch ja morgen am Haupteingang treffen und dann könnt ihr gemeinsam zum Chemieraum gehen? Laborausrüstung braucht man keine und das Chemiebuch bekommt Brian morgen direkt von Herrn Pötter, seinem Chemielehrer.

Du (auf Englisch zu Brian):

Brian: All right, thanks. So let's meet tomorrow morning at 7.50 in front of the main entrance. Could you please ask Mrs Meyer if I am allowed to use the German-English app on my smartphone in class? Without it, I am afraid that I won't understand very much.

Du (auf Deutsch zu Frau Meyer):

Frau Meyer: Ja, das verstehe ich. Also gut, Brian darf ausnahmsweise sein Smartphone benutzen – aber nur zum Nachschlagen von Wörtern! Du weißt ja, dass die Handynutzung ansonsten bei uns an der Schule verboten ist. Deshalb braucht er auch unbedingt eine Sondergenehmigung vom Schulleiter. Und er muss jeden Lehrer auch nochmal darüber informieren und um Erlaubnis bitten.

Du (auf Englisch zu Brian):

Brian: OK, thanks. So where can I find the headmaster?

Du (auf Deutsch zu Frau Meyer):

Frau Meyer: Aber das weißt du doch, einfach den Gang runter Richtung Sekretariat und dann die erste Tür rechts. Vielleicht gehst du da gleich in der Pause auch mit Brian zusammen hin und ihr klärt das? Vielen Dank, dass du dich so toll um Brian kümmerst! Ich muss jetzt auch mal wieder in den Unterricht. Wenn Brian noch weitere Fragen hat, kann er sich natürlich jederzeit an mich wenden!

Du (auf Englisch zu Brian):

Brian (zu Frau Meyer): OK, thanks, I will. Bye.

2. Compare your answers to the solution on p. 51 and fill in the following table.

Criteria	Evaluation of your mediation text: ☺ ☺ ☹	Comments
I included all the important information.		
I did not include any irrelevant information / too many details.		
I could understand the relevant information and express it in the other language.		
I considered the context, addressee(s) and purpose of the mediation task.		
I had no difficulty switching between English and German as required by the mediation task.		

Practise your competences

In the first part of this chapter you can practise specific skills required for successful mediation. These skills include getting into the communicative context, reading comprehension, listening comprehension, summarizing and paraphrasing, dealing with unknown words and false friends, and creating structure and coherence. You can either work through them one by one, or pick the skills most relevant for you on the basis of your self-evaluation from chapter 1.

The second part of this chapter contains step-by-step guided mediation tasks for English-German and German-English mediation on the basis of various texts and materials.

2.1 Skills practice

A   Getting into the communicative context

Mediation does not mean that you translate the given text word by word. Instead, you have to decide which information in the text is relevant in the mediation context. The following questions can help you to do so:

- **Addressee(s):** Who are you doing the mediation for? What does he/she know? What is he/she interested in?

- **Text type:** What type of text is the given text (for example, an email, a newspaper article, presentation, etc.)? Which text type are you supposed to produce?

- **Language:** What kind of language is used in the given text (for example, formal, informal, slang, literary, technical, etc.)? Can you use the same language in your mediation text?

- **Purpose:** What is the purpose or the aim of the given text (for example, warning, information, entertainment, etc.)? What is the purpose of your mediation text?

The following exercises will help you to understand different mediation tasks in order to decide which information to transmit in the given context.

a)   Understanding the mediation task and the given text

EXERCISE

Imagine that you have to mediate in the following tasks. Read the tasks carefully and compare the given text (i.e. the text that you are supposed to mediate) and the target text (your mediation text) with regard to addressee(s), text type, language and purpose. Then complete the table.

Task	Given text (Ausgangstext)		Target text (Zieltext)
Your Irish exchange partner Susan has to do a presentation in her geography class on a documentary about Berlin. Since her German is not very good, she has difficulty understanding it. *Write an email to your exchange partner Susan in which you summarize the documentary in English. (p. 9)*	Addressee(s):	all kinds of different people who are interested in the topic (i. e. tourism and waterways in Berlin)	
	Text type:	documentary	
	Language(s):		
	Purpose:		inform a teenage girl about the contents of the documentary so that she can present it to her classmates
Brian from London is a new exchange student in your class. Your teacher, Frau Meyer, asks you to help Brian and to show him his way around at your school. Unfortunately, Frau Meyer's English is not very good, and Brian does not speak much German yet. So you have to mediate from German to English for Frau Meyer and from English to German for Brian. (p. 11)	Addressee(s):	Brian (teenage boy) and Frau Meyer (teacher)	Brian (teenage boy) and Frau Meyer (teacher)
	Text type:	conversation	
	Language/s):		
	Purpose:	Frau Meyer: give Brian some information Brian: ask questions, get information	
Together with your cousin Christian, you are going to spend a few days in London. Since you and Christian live in different cities, you are writing each other emails about the trip. Christian is organizing the hotel, you are responsible for the sightseeing programme. On the internet you have found information about a sightseeing trip that you would like to inform your cousin about. (p. 39)	Addressee(s):	people interested in London sightseeing and ghost tours	
	Text type:		
	Language:		
	Purpose:	make tourists book the guided tour	
You are an exchange student at a boarding school in England. Your teacher has asked you to contribute an article for the school's student magazine. The topic is "Jobs and traineeships for young people in Germany". (p. 33)	Addressee(s):	newspaper readers interested in the topic	
	Text type:		
	Language:		
	Purpose:		inform English teenagers about the topic (i.e. training positions in Germany)

b) Respecting the requirements of your mediation text

Every type of text has a specific format, style and language. If your mediation has to be a certain text type, you have to be aware of these requirements in order to successfully accomplish the task.

EXERCISE

Match the following text types with the corresponding characteristic features.

Text type	Characteristic features (language, style, set phrases, format, length, etc.)
1. (Formal) letter	E. Informal language; contains personal information, experiences, opinions or attitudes; no set phrases; no formal requirements; may end with an invitation for comments
2. Email	C. Informal language (short forms, incomplete sentences, etc.); set phrases, no formatting requirements, symbols / emoticons allowed; not too long
3. Blog	F. On a film, theatre performance, book, text or work of art; often starts with a summary; gives personal opinion or recommendation
4. Newspaper article	H. Informal language; set phrases for starting, ending, turn-taking, clarifying, etc.
5. Review	A. Formal, polite language; set phrases (Dear Sir or Madam, etc.); not too long; divided into paragraphs
6. Conversation/ discussion	D. Informal language; set phrases for turn-taking, clarifying, etc.
7. Telephone conversation	B. Formal language; neutral style; not too long; divided into paragraphs; contains title, by-line (the author's name) and subheadings; frequent structure: "reverse triangle" (from more important to less important information)
8. Presentation	G. Formal language; no interaction; clear structure

1	2	3	4	5	6	7	8

B Reading comprehension

In order to successfully mediate a written text, you have to understand its main points and decide which information is relevant in the given mediation context. The following reading strategies can help you:

- **Skimming:** Looking at the text to quickly understand its main ideas (i. e. the gist). The following clues might help you:
    - title, subtitle, subheadings, illustrations, etc.,
    - the first and last sentences of each paragraph,
    - key words, words written in bold or italics.
- **Scanning:** Looking at the text to quickly identify specific information. Think of words, word families and key phrases related to the information you are looking for, then find and highlight them in the text.

TIP

Taking notes

- It does not matter which highlighting system (different colours, symbols, numbers, abbreviations, etc.) you use, as long as it is clear and you can still understand it later on. Before you start highlighting information in a given text, it is helpful to determine which aspects you want to focus on and how you are going to distinguish the different kinds of information.
- It might be helpful to visualize the information by re-structuring it, for example in a table, flowchart or diagram.
- You can use German, English or both for your notes, but German notes might tempt you to translate the text word for word rather than mediating it.

---

a) Skimming (basic level)

EXERCISES

1. Look at the text about Scotland on p. 17 (heading(s), picture, etc.) and write in one sentence (in German) what it is about.

2. Write one sentence (in German) for each paragraph saying what it is about.

DOCUMENT

WILDERNESS SCOTLAND
THE GREAT FAMILY ADVENTURE – TREASURE HIGHLANDS

The famous novel by Robert Louis Stevenson, Treasure Island, is perhaps the classic children's adventure story.

What a lot of people don't know is that it was written in the Cairngorms National Park in 1881!

With this in mind, we've designed this spectacular family adventure holiday, combining lots of activities, a treasure hunt, desert islands and the Cairngorms National Park, to create an adventure holiday which is sure to be a hit with all of the family. You will visit ruined castles, enjoy spectacular scenery and try activities including sea kayaking, canoeing and mountain biking as you explore the Scottish Highlands – a land of myths and legends.

Our guides are highly-qualified, so you can be sure that safety is a priority at all times – even though it will feel like an adventure! As well as being qualified to take people out into the wilds, our guides are also great with family groups – they enjoy introducing our clients to the local environment and helping them explore it. […]

You will spend 4 nights staying at a comfortable B&B in or close to the West Highland town of Fort William. You then move east to Cairngorms National Park for your final 2 nights. If you book a 2-night extension, you will stay in a B&B close to the Highland Games that you will be attending. A warm welcome is assured in these family friendly accommodations. Accommodation is in double, twin or family bedrooms, en-suite wherever it is available. Breakfast is included each morning. […]

This is a self-drive trip. You can bring your own car or hire from anywhere in Scotland. If you are hiring, the best place to start from is Inverness. For full details on how to get to Inverness, please see our website: Travel to Scotland

Quelle: https://www.wildernessscotland.com/adventure-holidays/family/great-family-adventure-treasure-highlands/ (zuletzt aufgerufen am 15.01.2018)
Foto: Fotolia / Nick Fox

What's included?
- 6 nights accommodation B & Bs
- Breakfast each day
- Lunch on Day 6
- Day 2: Return travel on the Harry Potter steam train
- Day 3: A day of guided sea kayaking (as part of a larger group), inc. all hire equipment
- Day 4: Private guiding on a canoeing and biking trip, plus all equipment hire
- Day 5: Half day of mountain biking, including bike hire
- Day 6: Full day of privately guided hiking and geocaching

Quelle: https://www.wildernessscotland.com/adventure-holidays/family/great-family-adventure-treasure-high-lands/ (zuletzt aufgerufen am 15.01.2018)

b) Scanning (advanced level)

EXERCISE

Scan the text on p. 17 for information that is particularly relevant for parents travelling with children. Highlight the corresponding key words and take notes (in German).

C Listening comprehension

When you listen to a text to mediate its content, you do not necessarily have to understand every word. Instead, the following two listening strategies are more helpful:

- **Listening for gist:** In order to understand the main point(s) of the text, try to gain information about medium, text type, source, title, speakers, context and topic to activate your pre-knowledge.
- **Listening for detail:** When you listen for specific details, you can prepare by:
  - thinking of key words and phrases (often names, times, numbers and places) related to this information and focus on those.
  - guessing where the information might be in the text and which speaker might provide it.

> ## TIP
>
> **Taking notes while listening**
> - Use key words, abbreviations and symbols to write as fast as possible.
> - Use simple language and avoid trying to write down words that you do not understand.
> - Use headings, numbers, bullets, etc. to structure your notes. Connectors within the listening text *(and, although, then, after, at last,* etc.) can help you to follow the structure of the text.
> - Leave space between the bullet points to add missing information later.
> - Look at your notes again directly after listening. Often you will still remember something or you can correct wrong or illegible points.

a) Listening for gist (basic level)

In the following you are going to listen to a documentary about body scanners at airports.

DOCUMENT

"Body scanners", Continuco / Cornelsen / ZDF Enterprises (2:51 min., see CD / Track 2)

EXERCISE

While listening for the first time, take some notes:

Where are the body scanners used?

According to the documentary, are body scanners a good or a bad thing?

b) Listening for detail (advanced level)

While you are listening to the documentary again, take more detailed notes on possible advantages of and problems with body scanners with regard to security and practicality (potential health risks, check-in speed and privacy). Fill in the table.

	Advantages	Problems
Security (prevention of terrorist attacks, etc.)		
Practicality (health risks, speed, privacy)		

D   Mediating in a conversation

Mediation during a conversation can be quite challenging because you have to consider at least two conversation partners and switch constantly between languages. The following exercises can help you to deal with these complex requirements.

SITUATION

In a snack bar in London you are mediating between your cousin Marie, who does not speak much English, and the shop assistant, who does not speak any German.

EXERCISES

1. In the following conversation the sentences are mixed up. Put them in the correct order by numbering them from 1 to 18.

Shop assistant: Hello. What can I do for you?
You: Sonst noch etwas?
Marie: Ich hätte gerne ein Sandwich.
Marie: Ja, ich hätte gerne noch Käse und Zwiebeln.
You: Alles klar. Er möchte wissen, was du gerne auf deinem Sandwich hättest.
Shop assistant: £3.05, please.

Marie: Ich hätte gerne ein Thunfisch-Sandwich mit Gurke.
Marie: Nein, danke. Wie viel kostet das?
You: She would like to have a tuna sandwich with cucumber.
You: Er fragt, was er für dich tun kann.
You: Er fragt, ob du noch etwas möchtest.
You: No, thanks. How much is it?
Shop assistant: OK. Is there anything else you would like?
You: She would like some cheese and onions as well.
You: She would like to have a sandwich.
Shop assistant: Sure, here you are. Anything else?
Shop assistant: All right. What would you like on your sandwich?
You: 3,05 Pfund.

2. Now take a coloured pen and highlight or underline everything the mediator says. Then compare these sentences with the original sentences that are mediated and complete the following table.

	Original sentence	Mediated sentence
Which pronouns (you, he, she, we, they, etc.) are used?		
What kind of sentences (statement, question, etc.) are used?		
What kind of speech (direct or indirect speech) is used?		

E   Summarizing and paraphrasing

To summarize a text means presenting all the essential information in a structured way. The following strategies can help you:

- Start your summary with information about the title, author, source and main topic
  (*"The text XX by XX, which appeared in XX, is about / deals with …"*).
- Divide the given text into paragraphs and structure your summary accordingly.
- Do not include information that is not essential (examples, illustrations, descriptive details). If you are not sure, ask yourself whether this piece of information is necessary to understand the text.
- Do not give your own opinion or interpretation.
- Use clear and neutral language (present tense, your own words, no figurative language, irony or direct quotes).
- References to person, time and place have to be altered (*I → he / she, yesterday → the day before, here → there,* etc.).
- Your summary should be between one quarter and one third of the original text.

a) Preparing a summary (basic level)

DOCUMENT

Internetsucht   30. Mai 2017

600 000 JUGENDLICHE GELTEN ALS INTERNETABHÄNGIG

Von Kristiana Ludwig, Berlin

Der Bielefelder Kinderarzt Uwe Büsching begegnet dem Anfang allen Übels in seiner eigenen Praxis. Es ist der Vater, der seinem Kind, wenn es Angst vor einer Spritze hat, kein Spielzeug mehr in die Hand gibt – sondern sein Handy und darauf ein Video abspielt. Oder die Mutter, die beim Stillen mit einer Hand ihr Kind hält und mit der anderen ihre E-Mails liest. Büsching ist im Berufsverband der Kinder- und Jugendärzte. 79 seiner Kollegen haben im vergangenen Jahr in 15 Bundesländern 5 600 Patienten untersucht und sie mit ihren Eltern gefragt, wie sie Smartphones und Tablets nutzen. Das Ergebnis ist eine erste umfangreiche Studie zu den gesundheitlichen Folgen des modernen Medienkonsums, in Auftrag gegeben von der Bundesdrogenbeauftragten Marlene Mortler (CSU).

Demnach gelten in Deutschland mittlerweile 600 000 Jugendliche und junge Erwachsene als internet-abhängig und zweieinhalb Millionen als problematische Internetnutzer. 70 Prozent der Kinder im Kita-Alter nutzen das Handy der Eltern mehr als eine halbe Stunde täglich, 90 Prozent von ihnen wer-

Quelle: http://www.sueddeutsche.de/gesundheit/internetsucht-jugendliche-gelten-als-internetabhaengig-1.3526050 (zuletzt aufgerufen am 15.01.2018)

den dabei nicht weiter kontrolliert. Dabei wirke sich Mutters Smartphone schon bei Kleinkindern auf die Gesundheit aus. Für einen Zusammenhang zwischen Fütter- und Einschlafstörungen bei Säuglingen und der Nutzung digitaler Medien der Eltern habe der beauftragte Kölner Medizin-ökonomie-Professor Rainer Riedel „signifikante Hinweise" gefunden. […] Bei Kindern zwischen zwei und fünf Jahren bringen die Wissenschaftler Hyperaktivität sowie Konzentrations- und Sprach-störungen mit ihrer Mediennutzung in Verbin-dung. […]

Quelle: http://www.sueddeutsche.de/gesundheit/internetsucht-jugendliche-gelten-als-internetabhaengig-1.3526050 (zuletzt aufgerufen am 15. 01. 2018)
Foto: Fotolia / Antonioguillem

EXERCISES

1. Read the text carefully, marking key words and dividing it into paragraphs.
2. Which of the following introductions is best suited to start a summary of the given text, and why?

Introductions	Your evaluation ☺ ☺ ☹	Reasons for your evaluation
1. The article is about the dangers of the internet for children.		
2. The article is about the dangers of smartphones for small children.		
3. The article is about parents' and children's use of modern communication media and its negative effects on the development of children and teenagers.		

b) Writing your own summary (advanced level)

After deciding which information to put into your summary, the next step is to express the information without copying from or, in the case of mediation, translating the original text. The following paraphrasing techniques can help you to do so:

- using synonyms / words with similar meanings *(to start → to begin)*,
- using antonyms / opposites *(to be honest → not lying)*,
- using general expressions *(a kind of …, something like …)* followed by a specification,
- simplifying, for example by making two sentences out of one very complex sentence,
- using general terms instead of examples and enumerations *(cucumbers, tomatoes and lettuce → vegetables)*,
- changing word categories *("Die Wahlbeteiligung war niedrig." → "Many people choose not to vote.")*.

EXERCISES

1. Use one of the techniques explained above to paraphrase the expressions from the newspaper article in a).

German expression	English paraphrase	Strategy used
soziale Medien		
internetabhängig		
problematische Internetnutzer		
sich auswirken auf		
Konzentrationsstörungen		
mit etwas in Verbindung bringen		

2. Now write your own summary of the given text, using your notes from a). Remember to use your own words (the expressions in the box below might help you.). The tips from section H (see p. 31) can help you to structure your summary.

media consumption · to be addicted to sth. (von etw. abhängig sein) · to be at risk (gefährdet sein) · health risks (gesundheitliche Risiken)

F   Dealing with unknown words

When mediating, you might be faced with English words, phrases or expressions that you do not understand, or German words that you cannot translate into English. In these cases, the use of a dictionary can be helpful, but also has some disadvantages:

Advantages	Risks
• Helpful for technical terms or subject-specific vocabulary • Necessary for direct translations • Can be helpful to find paraphrases, collocations or word fields	• Looking up words is time-consuming • Temptation of translating (thus giving too much detail) instead of mediating, i. e. using your own words • Danger of choosing wrong translations, especially when looking up individual words without considering the context

For mediation it is, therefore, often more helpful to try to guess unknown words first before using a dictionary. The following strategies can help you to do so:

● From the context and the position of the word within the sentence you can conclude its general meaning and word class.

● You might know words from the same word family (*to destroy → destruction*) or similar words from another language (*campaign – Kampagne; proposal – (the French verb) proposer*).

● Suffixes and prefixes often have the same or similar meanings in different words (*photograph-er / teach-er; dis-agreeable / dis-advantage*).

● Compounds are often made up of words you already know (*passer-by, post-war*).

a) Guessing the meaning of unknown words when mediating from English to German (basic level)

EXERCISE

Practise the strategies to guess the meaning of new words by completing the following table.

English word or expression	Strategy used	Meaning
to document	• other language (German: dokumentieren) • word family (noun: document)	dokumentieren
preparation		
unforgivable		
to come round		
dignified		
commercial		
justified		
entry		

b) Paraphrasing unknown words when mediating from German to English (advanced level)

The strategies for guessing unknown words from task a) can also be helpful to paraphrase German words in English. Additionally, you might find the following strategies helpful:

- Sometimes you can express a concept by a more general term which you can then specify further (*Adventskranz → a wreath decorated with stars, ribbons and four candles, which is used as a decoration in the weeks before Christmas*).

- Long German compound nouns can often be expressed with an of-phrase or a verbal phrase (*Liebesbeweis → a proof of one's love*).
- Looking for a German synonym might help you to find an English equivalent (*entlassen → feuern → to fire*).
- Remember that sometimes additional (contextual or cultural) information is necessary for your partner to understand a certain concept (for example to understand *Frauenparkplatz* the addressee needs to know about the prejudice that women are worse drivers than men).

EXERCISE

Practise the strategies to paraphrase difficult German expressions by completing the following table.

German word or expression	Strategy used	English word or expression
die Akzeptanz	● other language (French: acceptance) ● word family (verb: to accept)	acceptance
sicherheitsbewusst		
beispielhaft		
An- und Verkauf		
hoffnungsvoll		
hinterlassen		
Angebot		
reservieren		

G   Dealing with false friends

a) Being aware of false friends (basic level)

EXERCISE

Read the following newspaper article and answer the questions.

What are false friends?

Why is it important to avoid false friends?

IN DIESE SPRACH-FETTNÄPFCHEN TAPPEN DEUTSCHE GERN

Von Michael Hegenauer | Veröffentlicht am 14.11.2013

„Ich werde ein Bier"
„I become a beer." Ist der Deutsche durstig, sagt er in der Heimat gern „Ich bekomme ein Bier".
Überträgt er diese Aussage ins Englische und sagt zum Kellner „I become a beer", bedeutet das aber,
dass er sich in ein Bier verwandelt. Selbst für Harry Potter wäre das schwierig.

„Ein Auge zum Frühstück"
„I'd like an Ei for breakfast." Das deutsche Ei ist im Englischen ein „egg" – das Ei klingt in den Ohren
des Engländers nach „eye": das Auge. Das sollte man lieber nicht zum Frühstück bestellen.

„Können Sie meine Windeln wechseln"
„Can you change me?" Eigentlich möchte der Kunde fragen: „Können Sie mir bitte Geld wechseln?"
Mit „can you change me" fragt er aber, ob der nette Bankangestellte ihm die Windeln wechseln könne –
„can you change my money" wäre hier korrekt gewesen.

Praktisch und handlich: „handy"
Auch hier wurde auf die englische Sprache zurückgegriffen, ohne sich über die Bedeutung des Wortes
im Klaren zu sein: Das „Handy" der Deutschen kennen Amerikaner als „cell phone", der Engländer nennt
es „mobile phone". „Handy" ist hingegen ein Adjektiv und bedeutet „handlich" oder „praktisch". […]

Keine Vergiftungsgefahr
„I have a gift for you!" Wenn eine englischsprachige Person jemandem ein „gift" geben möchte, besteht
keine Gefahr für Leib und Leben, hier soll lediglich ein Geschenk überreicht werden.

Ein Felsen im Modegeschäft
„I am looking for a nice rock." Fern der Heimat macht Einkaufen doch am meisten Spaß – es schadet
auch nie, den Verkäufer um Hilfe zu bitten. Doch denkt der bei „rock" nicht an ein Bekleidungsstück,
sondern an einen Felsen. „Skirt" meint das Kleidungsstück.

Quelle: https://www.welt.de/reise/article121880750/In-diese-Sprach-Fettnaepfchen-tappen-Deutsche-gern.html (zuletzt aufgerufen am 15.01.2018)

b) Recognizing false friends (basic level)

EXERCISE

Complete the following table. You can add other false friends that have caused you difficulty in the past.

English word	German translation	False friend	English translation
actual	wirklich, tatsächlich, eigentlich	aktuell	topical, current, up-to-date
all day		alle Tage	
also		also	
brand		Brand	
to become		bekommen	
to blame sb.		sich blamieren	
brave		brav	
brief		Brief	
chips		Chips	
consequent		konsequent	
decent		dezent	
dose		Dose	
engaged		engagiert	
eventual(ly)		eventuell	
fabric		Fabrik	
fast		fast	
gift		Gift	
gymnasium		Gymnasium	
handy		Handy	
meaning		Meinung	
murder		Mörder	
must not		nicht müssen	
note		Note	
to probe		proben	

English word	German translation	False friend	English translation
prospect		Prospekt	
Roman		Roman	
self-conscious		selbstbewusst	
sensible		sensibel	
sympathetic		sympathisch	

c) Avoiding false friends (advanced level)

EXERCISES

1. Translate the following sentences into German.

My boss is actually more decent than I had thought.

You must not be too self-conscious.

I don't understand the meaning of this gift.

The plan to build a new gymnasium seemed quite sensible.

2. Translate the following sentences into English.

Er blamierte sich mit seiner Meinung.

Eventuell bekomme ich morgen einen wichtigen Brief.

Der Mörder schien eigentlich recht sympathisch.

Er hat sein Handy bei dem Brand verloren.

H   Creating structure and coherence

a) Expressions to create structure and coherence (basic level)

EXERCISE

Complete the following table with linking words and expressions from the box.

first (of all) · furthermore · because · however · It is true that … but … · finally ·
moreover · since · nevertheless · although · eventually · firstly · on top of that ·
therefore · in contrast to · even if · last but not least · in addition to (that) · so that ·
in order to · in spite of · in the end · to start with · secondly · as a result · the next
point · on the one hand …, on the other hand … · whereas · after that · while ·
in conclusion · then · above all · all in all · to conclude · consequently · even though ·
to sum up · in connection with · both … and … · in short · either … or … · moving on

Getting started:	
Adding new ideas:	
Giving reasons:	
Contradicting:	
Conceding:	
Concluding:	

b) Using linking words and expressions to improve a given text (advanced level)

EXERCISE

Improve the following text by rewriting it with some of the expressions from exercise a).

The "Bundesdrogenbeauftragte" (Federal Commissioner for Drugs) has commissioned the first extensive study on the health effects of modern media consumption in families conducted by German pediatricians.

According to the study, 600 000 teenagers are addicted to the internet. 2.5 million young people are in danger of becoming so. Many pre-school aged children use their parents' smartphones, often even without supervision.

Smartphone use can lead to health risks for toddlers. There seems to be a link between parents' digital media use and feeding and sleeping disorders in infants. In children between 2 and 5 years of age there seems to be a connection between their media habits and language as well as concentration problems.

2.2 Mediation practice

For most mediation tasks and contexts, it makes sense to go through the following basic steps:

1. Analysing the task
↓
2. Understanding the source
↓
3. Mediating
↓
4. Editing your text (only for written mediation)

The following exercises will help you to go through these steps for various mediation tasks on the basis of different spoken and written texts in German and in English. You can either go through them one by one or choose one type of task or topic that you want to practise in particular.

A   Ausbildungsplätze
(Mediation: German → English)

SITUATION

You are an exchange student at a boarding school in England. Your teacher has asked you to write an article for the school's student magazine. The topic is "Jobs and traineeships for young people in Germany".

DOCUMENT

SO VIELE OFFENE LEHRSTELLEN WIE NOCH NIE

Von Tina Groll   13. August 2016

Der Ausbildungsmarkt entwickelt sich zunehmend zu einem Bewerbermarkt. Das zeigen die jüngsten Daten der Bundesagentur für Arbeit. Demnach gab es 172 200 unbesetzte Ausbildungsplätze, aber nur 148 000 noch suchende Bewerberinnen und Bewerber. Das heißt, selbst wenn alle Bewerber eine Stelle finden, wären noch 24 200 Ausbildungsplätze unbesetzt. Noch nie waren zu Beginn des Ausbildungsjahres so viele Lehrstellen offen und noch nie war die rechnerische Lücke zwischen Nachfrage und Angebot so groß. Zum Vergleich: Im vergangenen Jahr suchten 4,2 Prozent mehr junge Männer und Frauen noch einen Ausbildungsplatz – und 5,5 Prozent weniger offene Stellen. [...]

Quelle: http://www.zeit.de/karriere/beruf/2016-08/ausbildungsmarkt-lehrstellen-bewerber-statistik (zuletzt aufgerufen am 15.01.2018)
Foto: Fotolia / Kzenon

Das liegt zum einen an der zunehmenden Akademisierung: Immer weniger junge Erwachsene verlassen die Schule mit einem Realschulabschluss, viele Schulabgänger hängen noch ein paar Schuljahre bis zur Fachhochschulreife oder dem Abitur dran. Zum anderen rücken mit der sogenannten Generation Z die geburtenschwachen Jahrgänge in den Arbeitsmarkt nach. Außerdem bleibt auch die Berufswahl der Jugendlichen weitgehend traditionell. Die jungen Männer und Frauen wählen vor allem klassische Handel- und Kaufmannsberufe. Besonders im Handwerk fehlt der Nachwuchs. [...]

Laut Bundesagentur für Arbeit gehörten zu den zehn gefragtesten Ausbildungsberufen Ende Juli der Kaufmannsberuf mit Schwerpunkt Büromanagement, gefolgt von einer Ausbildung zum Einzelhandelskaufmann oder zur Einzelhandelskauffrau sowie einer klassischen Verkäufer-Ausbildung oder eine Ausbildung zum Industriekaufmann oder zur Industriekauffrau.

Quelle: http://www.zeit.de/karriere/beruf/2016-08/ausbildungsmarkt-lehrstellen-bewerber-statistik (zuletzt aufgerufen am 15.01.2018)

EXERCISES

1. With the help of a dictionary, find the expressions to complete the following table. Do you know other words or expressions that might be relevant for the topic?

German	English
	traineeship
arbeitslos	
	unemployment
Jobsuche	
	job candidate
Arbeitsmarkt	
Nachfrage	
Realschulabschluss	General Certificate of Secondary Education (GCSE)
Fachhochschulreife	advanced technical college entrance qualification
Abitur	
	graduate
	retail
Bürokaufmann/-frau	office management assistant

2. Now read the newspaper article carefully and highlight the information that might be useful for your article in the school magazine.
3. On the basis of what you have highlighted in the text, decide which of the following information is important for the given task. Say why or why not.

Piece of information	Important? Reasons?
There are more vacancies than young people looking for a job or traineeship.	
There were 24 200 open training positions.	
Last year, 4.2 % more young men and women were looking for a training position, while there were 5.5 % fewer vacant positions.	
Currently there are more open training positions than ever.	
Young people mostly choose jobs in trade and business.	
The data on traineeships were published by the German "Bundesagentur für Arbeit."	
Jobs in office management are more popular than jobs in retail.	
The most popular traineeships are in office management, retail and trade.	

4. Summarize the article in your own words.

B   Ein Ausflug nach Tschernobyl
(Mediation: German → English)

SITUATION

Your exchange partner from Sweden is visiting you. Together you have listened to a documentary on tourism to Chernobyl. Since your exchange partner's German is not very good, he asks you to explain to him what the documentary was all about and whether it would be a good idea for you to visit Chernobyl.

DOCUMENT

"Ausflug nach Tschernobyl", Continuco / Cornelsen / ZDF Enterprises (2:51 min., see CD / Track 3)

EXERCISES

1. Brainstorm for a few minutes and make notes (in German or English): What do you know about atomic energy? Do you know what happened in Chernobyl?

2. With the help of a dictionary, find the expressions to complete the following table. Do you know other words or expressions that might be relevant for the topic?

German	English
Atomkraft	
	nuclear power plant
	radioactive
verstrahlt, verseucht	
Strahlung	
	restricted area
Beton	
	nuclear reactor
GAU (größter anzunehmender Unfall)	
	sarkophargus
Geisterstadt	
	catastrophe

3. Now listen to the documentary once and say whether the following statements are right, wrong or not in the text.

	right	wrong	not in the text
The nuclear incident in Chernobyl took place in 1986.			
Tourists can now go on guided bus tours to the restricted area around the former nuclear power plant.			
The bus tours to Chernobyl cost €100.			
The day trips to Chernobyl start in Kiev.			
The radiation around the former power plant is 10 times higher than usual.			
Chernobyl is located in Ukraine, in the former Soviet Union.			

4. Listen to the documentary again and take notes (in German): Which information are you going to give your exchange partner?

5. Go through your notes from exercise 4 and prepare and practise what you are going to tell your exchange partner (in English!). The words from exercise 2 might help you.

TIP

In oral mediation situations like conversations, discussions or presentations you should remember to

- take into account your partners' situation and background knowledge,
- watch your partners and check whether they understand you,
- react to possible questions or comprehension problems.

C Movie review: The Hunger Games (Mediation: English → German)

SITUATION

Together with your younger sister you would like to watch a movie. One of the movies to choose from is "The Hunger Games". On the internet you have found a review, but your sister does not speak much English.

DOCUMENT

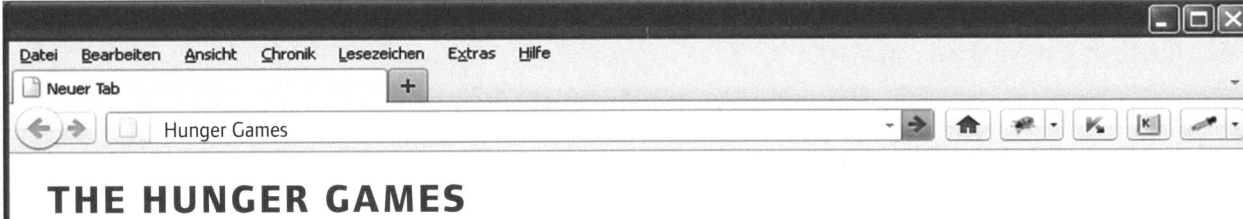

THE HUNGER GAMES

Olly Richards, 20 Mar 2009

In a future version of North America a small, wealthy city rules over the rest of the impoverished nation. Every year, a number of the country's youngest inhabitants are randomly selected to fight to the death in The Hunger Games. This year, Katniss Everdeen (Jennifer Lawrence) will change the game.

Probably the greatest achievement of The Hunger Games, and there are many, is that in adapting a phenomenally successful teen novel its creative team have produced something that works as a film, not just as an adaptation of a book. There's no required reading before entering the cinema in order to 'get it'. […] The Hunger Games as a novel has been dissected, expanded and retooled into something intelligent, immersive and powerfully current. […]

Jennifer Lawrence is perfect as Katniss. There's very little softness about her, more a melancholy determination that good must be done even if that requires bad things. […]

The violence and cruelty is most explicit in the Hunger Games arena, a vast, synthetic forest where 24 children hunt each other, and the level of brutality is very smartly done. You don't get a rating suitable for a teenage audience by gutting preteens or decorating the landscape with their blood. So Ross cuts around it. The constantly searching, handheld camerawork used throughout the film comes in most useful during moments of violence, flashing round the action and making you think you've seen everything without ever really clocking anything that would upset your appetite. […]

Quelle: https://www.empireonline.com/movies/hunger-games/review/ (zuletzt aufgerufen am 15.01.2018)

EXERCISES

1. Read the review carefully and mark the positive and/or negative aspects about the movie that are mentioned by the author.
2. Take notes (in German) on what you are going to tell your sister.

Worum geht es in dem Film?

Wie ist die Verfilmung gelungen im Vergleich zur Romanvorlage?

Was sagt der Rezensent über die Hauptdarstellerin?

Wie geht der Film mit Gewaltszenen um?

D London Ghost Walks (Mediation: English → German)

SITUATION

Together with your cousin Christian, you are going to spend a few days in London. Since you and Christian live in different cities, you are writing each other emails about the trip. Christian organizes the hotel, you are responsible for the sightseeing programme. On the internet you have found information about a sightseeing trip that you would like to inform your cousin about.

DOCUMENT

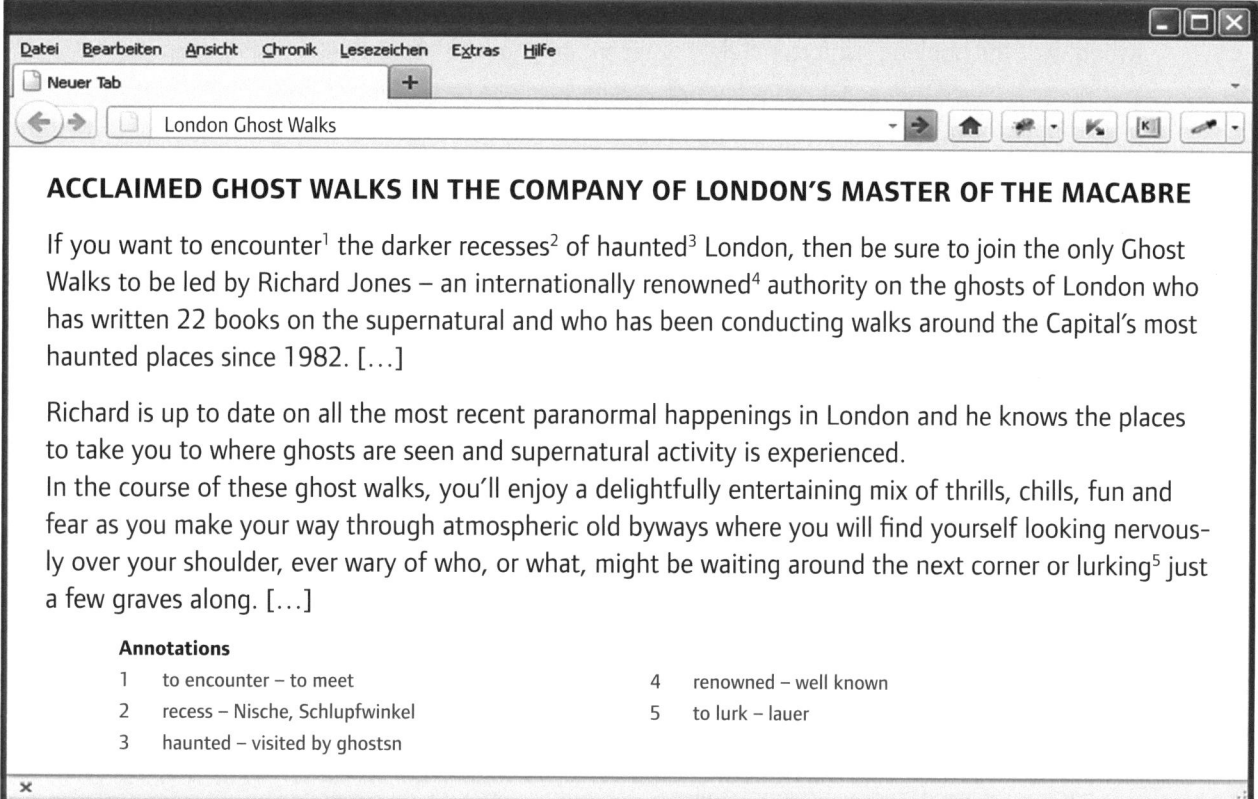

ACCLAIMED GHOST WALKS IN THE COMPANY OF LONDON'S MASTER OF THE MACABRE

If you want to encounter[1] the darker recesses[2] of haunted[3] London, then be sure to join the only Ghost Walks to be led by Richard Jones – an internationally renowned[4] authority on the ghosts of London who has written 22 books on the supernatural and who has been conducting walks around the Capital's most haunted places since 1982. [...]

Richard is up to date on all the most recent paranormal happenings in London and he knows the places to take you to where ghosts are seen and supernatural activity is experienced.
In the course of these ghost walks, you'll enjoy a delightfully entertaining mix of thrills, chills, fun and fear as you make your way through atmospheric old byways where you will find yourself looking nervously over your shoulder, ever wary of who, or what, might be waiting around the next corner or lurking[5] just a few graves along. [...]

Annotations

1	to encounter – to meet		4	renowned – well known
2	recess – Nische, Schlupfwinkel		5	to lurk – lauer
3	haunted – visited by ghostsn			

EXERCISES

1. Read the advertisement carefully and mark the information that you think will be interesting for your cousin.

2. Write the email to your cousin (in German). You can start as follows:

Hi Christian,

es gibt Neuigkeiten zu unserem London-Trip: Ich habe gerade eine coole Sightseeing-Tour gefunden:

Was meinst du, wollen wir das machen?

Gibt es schon Neuigkeiten wegen der Hotelbuchung? Bin gespannt, von dir zu hören!

Bis bald,

E   At the youth hostel (Mediation: English ↔ German)

SITUATION

Together with your youth group, you are on a trip to London. When the group leader telephones the youth hostel where your group is going to stay, it turns out that something went wrong with the booking. Unfortunately, the receptionist at the youth hostel does not speak any German. Since the leader of your youth group does not speak much English, he is quite upset. So you want to help by mediating between the two.

EXERCISES

1. Luckily, you have a few minutes before your arrival at the youth hostel. You can use this time to prepare for the mediation.

Write down all the (English!) words that come to mind when you think of (hotel/hostel) reservations and bookings:

Write down what could possibly go wrong with a group reservation at a youth hostel:

2. Now you are at the reception of the youth hostel. Mediate between your group leader and the receptionist. You can practise for this oral mediation situation by writing down your answers as spontaneously as possible.

Receptionist: Good afternoon. How can I help you?

You: We have made a reservation for nine boys, eight girls and two adults and you said on the phone that there is a problem with our reservation?

Receptionist: Yes, yes, I remember. I am sorry, but in the booking here it says you only have two four-bed-rooms for the boys. So we have no room for one of your boys …

You (in German, to your group's leader):

Group leader: Ich bin mir aber ganz sicher, dass ich bei der Buchung die genaue Anzahl der Teilnehmer mitgeteilt habe. Wie konnte denn das passieren?
You (in English, to the receptionist):

Receptionist: We are very sorry about our mistake. I was not here myself at the time your booking was made, so it was probably my new colleague. But I'll see what we can do for you.
You (in German, to your group's leader):

Receptionist: Well, another group just cancelled this morning. So there are now more three-bed-rooms available. Would it be okay for you to take three three-bed-rooms for the boys and two four-bed-rooms for the girls?
You (in German, to your group's leader):

Group leader: Ja, das würde doch gehen. Sind die denn dann teurer, als die Vierbettzimmer?
You (in English, to the receptionist):

Receptionist: Since it was our mistake and we are really sorry for the inconvenience, we won't charge you any extra costs for the extra room and the three-bed-rooms.
You (in German, to your group's leader):

Group leader: Okay, dann machen wir das so. Wann können wir die Räume beziehen?
You (in English, to the receptionist):

Receptionist: I will show you the rooms right now.

Test your competences

A   Things to do in Australia
(Mediation: English → German)

SITUATION

For her geography class your younger sister has to give a presentation on Australia. She has found a website with information. Since her English is not very good (and she is running out of time for the presentation), you have promised to help her.

DOCUMENT

THINGS TO DO IN AUSTRALIA

Australia may be big – we're talking the sixth largest country on the planet, stretching the same distance as Spain to western Russia – but it's not as daunting as it may seem. In fact, pick what you'd like to cover, and you can see the best of it in two weeks without any fears or worries.

Still not sure where to begin and what to see? Enter our Aussie Experts, who have not only curated a list of things to do in Australia, but created holiday itineraries to help you actually do them.

See the Great Barrier Reef
It's undoubtedly one of nature's greatest wonders. But don't just take our word for it – Sir David Attenborough also used the same phrase when he visited the Great Barrier Reef recently. If you watched him delve beneath the ocean's surface, you would have enjoyed just a glimpse at how spectacular this aquascape is. If you've snorkelled the reef in person, you'll know nothing can quite compare to being there. The sheer size alone of the reef will astound: all in, it covers 133 000 square miles and is home to 1 625 species of fish, 133 species of sharks and rays, 30 species of

whales and dolphins and 600 types of hard and soft coral. [. . .]

Visit Uluru
Australia's other famed icon, Uluru, is a monolith that's truly worthy of a visit. In fact never is Australia's vastness as palpable as it is on a Journey to the Red Centre. As the beating heart of the Outback, Uluru (also known as Ayers Rock) and the nearby town of Alice Springs is where life runs at a slower pace, wildlife flourishes and age-old Aboriginal culture endures. [. . .]

Drive along the Great Ocean Road
The Great Ocean Road is a scenic coastal highway which is part of a popular road trip that travels along Australia's southern coast between the cities of Melbourne and Adelaide. The road is famed for incredible scenery which includes rugged cliffs, the towering 12 Apostles, famous surf beaches and surrounding wineries. [. . .]

Watch wildlife on the Coral Coast
Located on the western coast of Australia, the Coral Coast is home to over 600 miles of pristine beaches, nature reserves and marine parks. As

Quelle: https://www.flightcentre.co.uk/travel-guides/australia/things-to-do (zuletzt aufgerufen am 15.01.208)
Foto: Fotolia / Rafael Ben-Ari

much of the region is protected, the Coral Coast is a veritable haven for wildlife watching, with common marine life sightings including dolphins, manta rays, turtles, whales, dugongs, coral and most notably, whale sharks. In fact the Coral Coast is one of the few places in the world where you can swim with the world's largest fish. Another famous animal unique to the Coral Coast is the quokka, a very cute and photogenic marsupial which can be seen when visiting Rottnest Island. […]

TASKS

1. Sum up the article for your sister (in German).

2. Evaluate your summary with the help of the solution on p. 62.

Criteria	Evaluation of your mediation text: ☺ ☺ ☹	Comments
I included all the important information.		
I did not include any irrelevant information / too many details.		
I did not have any language difficulties (words or expressions I did not know or could not express in the other language, etc.)		
I could understand the relevant information and express it in the other language.		
I used paragraphs and linking words to structure my summary.		

B Parapark Frankfurt – Erlebnistest
(Mediation: German → English)

SITUATION

Your penfriend Laura from Italy is going to visit you. Since she does not speak much German and you do not speak any Italian, you communicate in English. During her visit, you would like to go to Parapark with her.

DOCUMENT

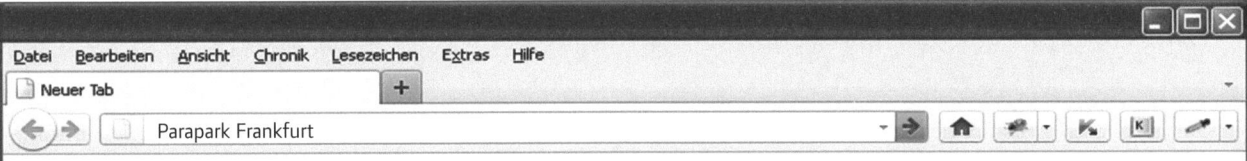

PARAPARK FRANKFURT LIVE ESCAPE GAME – ERLEBNISTEST

Von Jan Stein am 15. April 2016

Nachdem ich in Berlin schon so viele Live Escape Games testen durfte, hat es mich nach Frankfurt gezogen, denn da gibt es Parapark, das Urgestein unter den Live Escape Games in Deutschland. Ich habe mich schon lange auf den Besuch gefreut und nun war es endlich so weit.

Appartement 113 – Der Klassiker

Unser Team besteht heute aus 5 Leuten und wir haben natürlich vor, das **Appartement 113** zu knacken. Der Raum ist dem ersten originalen Live Escape Game aus Budapest nachempfunden. Alle meine Teamkollegen haben noch nie zuvor ein Live Escape Game gespielt. Darum wird es umso spannender, was uns heute erwartet.

Wir befinden uns in einem Hausflur wieder und neben uns sind **zwei verschlossene Wohnungstüren.** Eigentlich wollen wir so schnell wie möglich heraus, doch die Eingangstür ist ebenso fest verschlossen. Wir machen uns also auf die Suche nach dem Schlüssel nach draußen.

Das erste Rätsel ist sehr einfach zu lösen und schon befinden wir uns in einer der beiden Wohnungen. Hier suchen wir erst mal nach **Hinweisen und Gegenständen,** die uns weiterbringen sollen. Insgesamt gibt es viele verschiedene Rätsel und Aufgaben und einige habe ich schon mal vorher gesehen. Man sieht also, woher die anderen Anbieter teilweise ihre Ideen genommen haben.

Dennoch ist der Raum knifflig und **nur mit gutem Teamwork** und ein paar hilfreichen Tipps von unserer Game Masterin schaffen wir es, das Appartement 113 zu lösen und am Ende wieder zu entkommen.

Die Deko der Räume ist recht schlicht, sodass man nicht überfordert ist. Der Fokus liegt hier klar auf den Rätseln. Trotzdem kann durch das **Sounddesign** und die typische Rätsel-Musik eine spannende Atmosphäre aufgebaut werden. Jetzt weiß ich, warum das Appartement als der Klassiker schlechthin gesehen wird.

Mein Team und ich hatten so viel Spaß, dass wir direkt noch den anderen Raum, das 9. Portal, ausprobieren wollen. [...]

Quelle: http://www.lebegeil.de//parapark-frankfurt-das-live-escape-game (zuletzt aufgerufen am 15. 01. 2018)
Foto: Fotolia / domagoj8888

TASKS

1. Read the blogpost carefully and highlight information on what Parapark is and why it might be interesting for you and Laura.

2. Write an email to your friend Laura in which you explain the concept of Parapark and why you would like to go there with her. You can start as follows:

Dear Laura,

Your visit is coming closer and I am already planning some fun activities for us. One of them, I think, will be Parapark Frankfurt. I have read an article by a young blogger who tested the game with some friends. According to the author

What do you think? Would you like to go there?

I am already looking forward to seeing you!

Best wishes,

Your friend

3. Evaluate your text with the help of the solution on p. 63.

Criteria	Evaluation of your mediation text: ☺ ☺ ☹	Comments
I included all the important information.		
I did not include any irrelevant information / too many details.		
I could understand the relevant information and express it in the other language.		
I considered the context, addressee(s) and purpose of the mediation task.		
I used paragraphs and linking words to structure my email.		

C Boarding schools for international students (Mediation: English → German)

SITUATION

You would like to spend a year at a boarding school for international students, but you are afraid that your parents might be against it.

DOCUMENT

BOARDING SCHOOLS FOR INTERNATIONAL STUDENTS

November 16, 2015

Choosing the right boarding school for your child can be a challenging experience. With countless institutions on offer worldwide, and varying fees from the manageable to the superstellar, increased cost doesn't always result in quality. Parents are bombarded with options, all while trying to find the ideal home-away-from-home which combines modern facilities with excellent pastoral care in a community environment. Increasingly, prestigious institutions around the globe are opening their doors to international students, offering excellent academic teaching with manageable fees.

Lasting friendships

Children and teenagers can enjoy an excellent education while experiencing a new culture and creating lifelong friendships. From sports to art and drama to music, students can form lasting friendships and familial-style bonds while learning a new skill or attribute. In fact, increasing numbers of parents are choosing a boarding school education for their children as it enables them to gain internationally recognized qualifications while learning how to build relationships with their peers during a child's important formative years.

International boarding schools are accustomed to the initial teething problems posed by homesickness and culture shock, meaning that each student is provided with specialized care and support during their first few weeks when everything feels new and friendships are established. [...]

Spreading their wings

Furthermore, a boarding school education will encourage students to become more independent, from managing their belongings, class timetable and even getting out of bed to make it to lessons, children soon become self-sufficient, driven individuals with excellent time management skills. [...]

Professional career focus

Choosing an international boarding school education for your child can help set them on a dynamic career path from a very young age. Boarding schools recognize and hone childrens' talents, supporting and encouraging them during their school life. Parents can be assured that boarding schools often possess links to world renowned universities and institutions. From Cambridge to Yale, choosing an international boarding school will continue to

Quelle: https://www.studyinternational.com/news/5-top-boarding-schools-for-international-students/#ijfekfrCLX4QQMfl.97 (zuletzt aufgerufen am 15. 01. 2018)
Foto: Fotolia / Monkey

open doors within your child's educational and professional life.

Furthermore, international boarding schools offer activities which encourage students to learn and develop CV building skills alongside their full-time studies. Public speaking, debating society and even the chance to become a student prefect teach children responsibility and professional relationships, placing them at a distinct advantage in the student talent pool. Combining a traditional experience and high-calibre education ensures that international boarding schools produce well-rounded, talented individuals who stand out from the crowd. [...]

TASKS

1. Read the article carefully and highlight information that might be relevant to convince your parents.

2. Prepare a presentation for your parents (in German): Sum up the arguments for a stay at an international boarding school provided by the article.

3. Evaluate your presentation with the help of the solution on p. 63.

Criteria	Evaluation of your mediation text: ☺☺☺	Comments
I included all the important information.		
I did not include any irrelevant information / too many details.		
I could understand the relevant information and express it in the other language.		
I considered the context, addressee(s) and purpose of the mediation task.		
I used paragraphs and linking words to structure my presentation.		

D On holiday in Brighton
(Mediation: English ↔ German)

SITUATION

Your uncle has invited you on a trip to England. When checking into your first hotel in Brighton, you have to mediate between the receptionist, who does not speak any German, and your uncle, who does not speak any English.

TASKS

1. Mediate from German to English for the receptionist and from English to German for your uncle.

Receptionist: Good afternoon. How can I help you?

You: Do you have any rooms for us, please? We haven't made a reservation.

Receptionist: Yes, there are still some rooms available. How long would you like to stay?

You (to your uncle, in German):

Your uncle: Wollten wir nicht drei Tage bleiben und dann an der Küste weiter Richtung Cornwall?

You (to the receptionist, in English):

Receptionist: Great. Which rooms would you like? We have single bedrooms, double bedrooms with a king size bed and twin bedrooms with two individual beds. And you can have the rooms with bathrooms or with bathrooms in the hall.

You (to your uncle, in German):

Your uncle: Hm, keine Ahnung. Das kommt ja auch auf den Preis an. Frag doch mal bitte, wie viel die Zimmer kosten.

You (to the receptionist, in English):

Receptionist: The single is £45, the double or the twin room £75 a night. The rooms with the bathrooms in the hall are available for £30 the single and £60 the double and twin bedrooms.

You (to your uncle, in German):

Your uncle: Puh, ganz schön teuer … Ist das dann mit oder ohne Frühstück?

You (to the receptionist, in English):

Receptionist: Continental breakfast is included, full English breakfast costs £10 per person.

You (to your uncle, in German):

Your uncle: Ich denke, das normale Frühstück reicht, oder was meinst du? Dann nehmen wir am besten das Doppelzimmer mit den zwei getrennten Betten mit eigenem Badezimmer. Und am besten mit Meerblick.

You (to the receptionist, in English):

Receptionist: Unfortunately the only free rooms with sea view are single and double bedrooms.

You (to your uncle, in German):

Your uncle: Nein, also diese Doppelbetten hier in England sind mir zu eng. Dann nehmen wir doch lieber den Raum ohne Meerblick. Welche Etage ist der denn, und gibt es hier einen Aufzug?

You (to the receptionist, in English):

Receptionist: The room is on the third floor and you can use the lift over there. So, could you please fill in these forms for me?

You (to your uncle, in German):

2. Evaluate your answers with the help of the solution on p. 64.

Criteria	Evaluation of your mediation text: ☺ ☹ ☹	Comments
I included all the important information.		
I did not include any irrelevant information / too many details.		
I could understand the relevant information and express it in the other language.		
I considered the context, addressee(s) and purpose of the mediation task.		
I had no difficulty switching between English and German as required by the mediation task.		

Solutions and model answers

1 Check your mediation skills

A English language vacation
(Mediation: English → German)

Dauer und Kosten der Sprachkurse?
- 1–3 Wochen
- 410 Pfund pro Woche

Welche Leistungen sind im Preis eingeschlossen?
- 20 Unterrichtsstunden (15 Zeitstunden) pro Woche
- Lehrbuch
- ein Ganztags- und ein Halbtagsausflug pro Woche
- Nachmittagsaktivitäten
- Abendaktivitäten
- Lunchpaket

Weitere Vorteile der Junior Vacation am Brighton Language College?
- internationale Gruppen
- Unterricht in kleinen Gruppen (13 bis max. 16 Schüler)
- komplettes Programm mit Unterricht, Aktivitäten und sozialen Events
- Unterbringung in ausgewählten Gastfamilien

B Spaß im Stau
(Mediation: German → English)

Reiseziel-ABC ("Destination ABC")
For each letter of the alphabet you have to find something that goes with the place you are travelling to or from.

Kennzeichen-Sätze ("Registration Plate Sentences")
Make sentences with the letters on registration plates.

Weiterreden ("Keep talking")
One player starts with a word that consists of two parts, for example "sunglasses". The next player has to find a new word with the last part of the first word, for example "glass door".

Kettengeschichte ("Chain story")
The first player starts with a sentence, for example: "Once upon a time, there was a girl." Then the next player adds a sentence, and so the story goes on until you are tired of it or have reached your destination.

C Berlin – Hauptstadt am Wasser
(Mediation: German → English)

General information on Berlin's waterways:
- biggest rivers: Spree and Havel
- 200 km of navigable waterways and around 1000 bridges; one of the European cities with the most water

Information on Wannsee and Strandbad Wannsee:
- fine sandy beach, 1.2 km long
- 10 000s of visitors in the summer
- the public swimming pools were built in the 1920s

Information on the boat tour from Wannsee to Museumsinsel:
- starts next to Strandbad Wannsee and ends at the Museumsinsel
- on the Havel and Spree
- takes three hours
- many sights along the way: examples of modern architecture, the Federal Chancellor's Office, Berlin Central Station, Museumsinsel

**Transcript: „Berlin – Hauptstadt am Wasser",
Deutsche Welle, 24.05.2017**
Eine Reise entlang Berlins Wasserstraßen könnte auch hier beginnen: am Strandbad Wannsee. Zehntausende tummeln sich im Sommer am feinen Sandstrand. Der Wannsee bekommt sein Wasser von der Havel, neben der Spree Berlins größtem Fluss.
Die Badeanstalt im Stil der Neuen Sachlichkeit wurde in den 20er Jahren des letzten Jahrhunderts erbaut und steht unter Denkmalschutz.
Axel Ott war über 40 Jahre der Chef hier. Der ehemalige Bademeister ist vermutlich immer noch der größte Fan der Anlage:
„Der Sand ist fast karibisch, wir haben einen über 1,2 Kilometer langen Sandstrand. Wenn Sie hier abends den Sonnenuntergang sehen am Strandbad Wannsee, da gehen Sie hier über Schwanenwerder runter, dann stornieren Sie Ihren Urlaub und holen sich sofort am nächsten Tag 'ne Dauerkarte und werden hier Stammgast."
Oder ihr fahrt erst einmal weiter in die Stadt. Von der Anlegestelle neben dem Strandbad geht es drei Stunden lang über die Flüsse Havel und Spree bis ins Zentrum von Berlin.
Rund 200 Kilometer schiffbare Wasserstraßen und rund 1 000 Brücken. Berlin ist eine der wasserreichsten Städte Europas, meint Kapitän Immo Seeliger. Er fährt seit über 30 Jahren auf Berliner Gewässern.
„Berlin ist aus einem Kahn erbaut. Das heißt, die ganzen Baumaterialien wurden nach Berlin hingebracht und wurden

gebaut dadurch und … Ja, Berlin ohne Wasser kann man sich nicht vorstellen."

Nach zwei Stunden nähert ihr euch dem Zentrum. Auf dem Weg viel moderne Architektur. Nach der Wiedervereinigung gab es einen richtigen Bauboom an den Ufern der Spree.

Und hier hat Angela Merkel ihren Schreibtisch: das Bundeskanzleramt. Es war das erste Gebäude im heutigen Regierungs- und Parlamentsviertel.

Und schräg gegenüber der Hauptbahnhof.

Am Ziel, an der Museumsinsel, lohnt es sich, von Bord zu gehen und dem Ruf der Musik zu folgen. In der Strandbar Mitte gibt es zwar keinen Sandstrand, aber dafür regelmäßige Tanzveranstaltungen. Genau das Richtige für einen Sommerabend in Berlin.

© Deutsche Welle 2017

D The new exchange student (Mediation: English ↔ German)

Du (auf Englisch zu Brian): School starts at 8 am every day. Tomorrow your first lesson will be chemistry. So you can go straight to the chemistry lab.

Du (auf Deutsch zu Frau Meyer): Okay, er wird es versuchen, aber er möchte wissen, wo der Chemieraum ist und ob er irgendwelche Bücher oder Laborausrüstung benötigt.

Du (auf Englisch zu Brian): The chemistry lab is on the other side of the school, directly on the left of the main entrance. Maybe we could meet up tomorrow morning at the main entrance and go to the chemistry lab together? You don't need any lab equipment, and Mr. Pötter, your chemistry teacher, will give you the book tomorrow.

Du (auf Deutsch zu Frau Meyer): Darf Brian seine Übersetzungsapp auf dem Smartphone im Unterricht benutzen? Ohne versteht er leider noch nicht so viel.

Du (auf Englisch zu Brian): In this exceptional case you are allowed to use your smartphone in class, but only to look up translations! Usually students are not allowed to use their smartphones here at school. So you will need special permission from the headmaster. And you have to ask all your teachers if they are okay with it.

Du (auf Deutsch zu Frau Meyer): Er möchte wissen, wo er den Schulleiter finden kann.

Du (auf Englisch zu Brian): It's right over there, down the corridor towards the secretary's office, and then the first door on the right. But maybe we can go there together during the first break. Mrs Meyer has to go back to her class now. But she says you can always come to her if you have any other questions.

2 Practise your competences

2.1 Skills practice

A Getting into the communicative context

a) Understanding the mediation task and the given text

Task		Given text (Ausgangstext)	Target text (Zieltext)
Your Irish exchange partner Susan has to do a presentation in her geography class on a documentary about Berlin. Since her German is not very good, she has difficulty understanding it. *Write an email to your exchange partner Susan in which you summarize the documentary in English. (p. 9)*	Addressee(s):	all kinds of different people who are interested in the topic (i.e. tourism and waterways in Berlin)	Irish teenager
	Text type:	documentary	email
	Language(s):	German	English
	Purpose:	inform the audience about Berlin's water attractions	inform a teenage girl about the contents of the documentary so that she can present it to her classmates

	Addressee(s):	Brian (teenage boy) and Frau Meyer (teacher)	Brian (teenage boy) and Frau Meyer (teacher)
Brian from London is a new exchange student in your class. Your teacher, Frau Meyer, asks you to help Brian and to show him his way around at your school. Unfortunately, Frau Meyer's English is not very good, and Brian does not speak much German yet. So you have to mediate from German to English for Frau Meyer and from English to German for Brian. (p. 9)	Text type:	conversation	conversation
	Language/s:	German (Frau Meyer), English (Brian)	German (Frau Meyer), English (Brian)
	Purpose:	Frau Meyer: give Brian some information Brian: ask questions, get information	help Brian and Frau Meyer communicate with each other
Together with your cousin Christian, you are going to spend a few days in London. Since you and Christian live in different cities, you are writing each other emails about the trip. Christian is organizing the hotel, you are responsible for the sightseeing programme. On the internet you have found information about a sightseeing trip that you would like to inform your cousin about. (p. 39)	Addressee(s):	people interested in London sightseeing and ghost tours	your cousin (German teenager)
	Text type:	advertisement, website	email
	Language:	English	German
	Purpose:	encourage tourists to book the guided tour	inform Christian of the tour
You are an exchange student at a boarding school in England. Your teacher has asked you to write an article for the school's student magazine. The topic is "Jobs and traineeships for young people in Germany". (p. 33)	Addressee(s):	newspaper readers interested in the topic	British teenagers reading the school magazine
	Text type:	newspaper article	school magazine article
	Language:	German	English
	Purpose:	inform readers about the topic	inform English teenagers about the topic (i.e. training positions in Germany)

b) Respecting the requirements of your mediation text

1	2	3	4	5	6	7	8
A	C	E	B	F	D	H	G

B Reading comprehension

a) Skimming (basic level)

1. Im Text geht es um eine familienfreundliche Abenteuerrundfahrt durch die schottischen Highlands mit dem eigenen Auto oder einem Mietwagen.

2. Abschnitt 1: Die Abenteuerrundfahrt durch die schottischen Highlands bietet zahlreiche Aktivitäten, Sehenswürdigkeiten und spektakuläre Landschaften.
   Abschnitt 2: Die Reiseführer sind gut ausgebildet und erfahren darin, Besucher und vor allem Familien durch die wilden Gegenden zu führen und für ihre Sicherheit zu sorgen.

Abschnitt 3: Die Reisenden übernachten in zwei oder drei verschiedenen familienfreundlichen B & Bs in Doppeloder Familienzimmern, das Frühstück ist inklusive.

Abschnitt 4: Die Teilnehmer fahren selbst, entweder in ihrem eigenen Auto oder in einem Mietwagen.

b) Scanning (advanced level)

The famous novel by Robert Louis Stevenson, Treasure Island, is perhaps the classic children's adventure story. What a lot of people don't know is that it was written in the Cairngorms National Park in 1881!

With this in mind, we've designed this spectacular family adventure holiday, combining lots of activities, a treasure hunt, desert islands and the Cairngorms National Park, to create an adventure holiday which is sure to be a hit with all of the family. You will visit ruined castles, enjoy spectacular scenery and try activities including sea kayaking, canoeing and mountain biking as you explore the Scottish Highlands – a land of myths and legends.

Our guides are highly-qualified so you can be sure that safety is a priority at all times – even though it will feel like an adventure! As well as being qualified to take people out into the wilds, our guides are also great with family groups – they enjoy introducing our clients to the local environment and helping them explore it. [...]

You will spend 4 nights staying at a comfortable B & B in or close to the West Highland town of Fort William. You then move east to Cairngorms National Park for your final 2-nights. If you book a 2-night extension, you will stay in a B & B close to the Highland Games that you will be attending. A warm welcome is assured in these family friendly accommodations. Accommodation is in double, twin or family bedrooms, en-suite wherever it is available. Breakfast is included each morning. [...]

This is a self-drive trip. You can bring your own car or hire from anywhere in Scotland. If you are hiring, the best place to start from is Inverness. For full details on how to get to Inverness, please see our website: Travel to Scotland.

What's included?
- 6 nights accommodation B & Bs
- Breakfast each day
- Lunch on Day 6
- Day 2: Return travel on the Harry Potter steam train
- Day 3: A day of guided sea kayaking (as part of a larger group), inc all hire equipment
- Day 4: Private guiding on a canoeing and biking trip, plus all equipment hire
- Day 5: Half day of mountain biking, including bike hire
- Day 6: Full day of privately guided hiking and geo-caching

Notes in German:
- Programm: viele verschiedene Aktivitäten, Schatzsuche und einsame Inseln
- Aktivitäten: Kajak- und Kanufahren, Mountainbiken, Fahrradfahren, Wandern, Geocaching, Fahrt mit der Harry-Potter-Dampfeisenbahn
- die Gruppenführer haben Erfahrung mit Familien
- familienfreundliche Unterkünfte
- man legt die Strecken selbst im Auto zurück

C Listening comprehension

a) Listening for gist (basic level)

Where are the body scanners used?
Hamburg airport (test phase), in many other countries.

According to the documentary, are body scanners a good or a bad thing?
Most passengers look favourably upon the new technology, security standards are being met.

b) Listening for detail (advanced level)

	Advantages	Problems
Security (prevention of terrorist attacks, etc.)	• Hidden dangerous objects can be detected. • Body scanners recognize all kinds of potentially dangerous materials.	• It is still possible to smuggle dangerous objects under layers of moist cloth.
Practicality (health risks, speed, privacy)	• No health risk because they do not penetrate deep into the skin. • Body scanners are faster than traditional security checks.	• When body scanners are too sensitive, they slow down security checks. • People other than airport security personnel might get access to sensitive data.

Transcript: "Body scanners", Continuco / Cornelsen / ZDF Enterprises

The security check before departure is an unavoidable part of modern day air travel. For some weeks now two new body scanners have been in action in Hamburg for the first time in Germany. More than 100 000 passengers have been scanned in that time. Most air travellers look favourably upon this new technology.

Body scanners are part of ever more stringent security measures at airport terminals. Since the September 11 terrorist attacks they have become particularly sensitive. When a passenger smuggled plastic explosives onto a plane in his underwear, it was clear that this technology had to be improved.

And body scanners were the solution. They show stick figures and suspicious coloured areas.

Peter Schaar, federal data protection agent: "The technical measures are very reliable, but it is crucial that there be a discretion zone around the area of the scanner so that only security personnel can view the monitors. Even if the depictions are only rough Lego-like figures, it still isn't anybody else's business if a bunch of coloured areas are shown around a person's genital area."

It appears that these criteria are being met, at least in Hamburg. Body scanner technology irradiates the skin. However, in contrast to X-rays, which penetrate deep into the human body and must therefore be used only sparingly, these modern machines employ sub-millimetre radiation. This type of radiation is said to pose no risk to people's health as it does not pass through the moist epidermal layer of the human body.

This is why a weapon that British investigative journalists hid under several moist cutlets was not recognized by a body scanner.

The first body scanners were called full-body scanners because they showed lifelike images of a person's body. The models that are in use now are more advanced and offer more security.

Thomas de Maizière, Defence Minister: "These new body scanners recognize all materials that are located on someone's person and they therefore provide better security."

As always, passengers flying out of Hamburg are still submitted to traditional security checks. Going through the body scanner is voluntary in the test phase. The hope is that this technology will make security checks faster and more pleasant than a pat-down. However, the initial impression is that these machines are too sensitive and actually end up slowing down security checks on passengers. Body scanners are already being employed in many countries.

D   Mediating in a conversation

1.

1	Shop assistant: Hello. What can I do for you?
2	You: Er fragt, was er für dich tun kann.
3	Marie: Ich hätte gerne ein Sandwich.
4	You: She would like to have a sandwich.
5	Shop assistant: All right. What would you like on your sandwich?
6	You: Alles klar. Er möchte wissen, was du gerne auf deinem Sandwich hättest.
7	Marie: Ich hätte gerne ein Thunfisch-Sandwich mit Gurke.
8	You: She would like to have a tuna sandwich with cucumber.

9	Shop assistant: OK. Is there anything else you would like?
10	You: Er fragt, ob du noch etwas möchtest.
11	Marie: Ja, ich hätte gerne noch Käse und Zwiebeln.
12	You: She would like some cheese and onions as well.
13	Shop assistant: Sure, here you are. Anything else?
14	You: Sonst noch etwas?
15	Marie: Nein, danke. Wie viel kostet das?
16	You: No, thanks. How much is it?
17	Shop assistant: £3.05, please.
18	You: 3,05 Pfund.

2.

	Original sentence	Mediated sentence
Which pronouns (*you, he, she, we, they*, etc.) are used?	All pronouns possible, but mostly first person (*I, we / ich, wir*)	All pronouns possible, but mostly third person (*he, she, it, they / er, sie, es, sie*)
What kind of sentences (statement, question, etc.) are used?	All types of sentences possible	(Direct and indirect) statements and questions
What kind of speech (direct or indirect speech) is used?	Direct speech	Direct and indirect speech

E   Summarizing and paraphrasing

a)   Preparing a summary (basic level)

1. Der Bielefelder Kinderarzt Uwe Büsching begegnet dem Anfang allen Übels in seiner eigenen Praxis. Es ist der Vater, der seinem Kind, wenn es Angst vor einer Spritze hat, kein Spielzeug mehr in die Hand gibt – sondern sein Handy und darauf ein Video abspielt. Oder die Mutter, die beim Stillen mit einer Hand ihr Kind hält und mit der anderen ihre E-Mails liest.

Büsching ist im Berufsverband der Kinder- und Jugendärzte. 79 seiner Kollegen haben im vergangenen Jahr in 15 Bundesländern 5600 Patienten untersucht und sie mit ihren Eltern gefragt, wie sie Smartphones und Tablets nutzen. Das Ergebnis ist eine erste umfangreiche Studie zu den gesundheitlichen Folgen des modernen Medienkonsums, in Auftrag gegeben von der Bundesdrogenbeauftragten Marlene Mortler (CSU).

Demnach gelten in Deutschland mittlerweile 600000 Jugendliche und junge Erwachsene als internetabhängig und zweieinhalb Millionen als problematische Internetnutzer. 70 Prozent der Kinder im Kita-Alter nutzen das Handy der Eltern mehr als eine halbe Stunde täglich, 90 Prozent von ihnen werden dabei nicht weiter kontrolliert. Dabei wirke sich Mutters Smartphone schon bei Kleinkindern auf die Gesundheit aus. Für einen Zusammenhang zwischen Fütter- und Einschlafstörungen bei Säug-

lingen und der Nutzung digitaler Medien der Eltern habe der beauftragte Kölner Medizinökonomie-Professor Rainer Riedel „signifikante Hinweise" gefunden. [...] Bei Kindern zwischen zwei und fünf Jahren bringen die Wissenschaftler Hyperaktivität sowie Konzentrations- und Sprachstörungen mit ihrer Mediennutzung in Verbindung. [...]

2.

Introductions	Your evaluation	Reasons for your evaluation
1. The article is about the dangers of the internet for children.		• The article is not only about children using the internet but also about parents' use of communication media in general. • The negative consequences of media use are missing.
2. The article is about the dangers of smartphones for small children.		• The article is not only about smartphones but media use in general. • The dangers of parents' and teenagers' media habits are also mentioned.
3. The article is about parents' and children's use of modern communication media and its negative effects on the development of children and teenagers.		• This introduction includes both parents and children. • It mentions the negative effects of media habits.

b) Writing your own summary (advanced level)

1.

German expression	English paraphrase	Strategy used
soziale Medien	communication media	synonyms
internetabhängig	addicted to the internet	paraphrase
problematische Internetnutzer	internet users who are in danger of becoming addicted to the internet	general expression followed by specification
sich auswirken auf	to have consequences for	change of word categories
Konzentrationsstörungen	not being able to concentrate	antonyms
mit etwas in Verbindung bringen	to link sth. to	simplification, change of word categories

2. The article is about parents' and children's use of modern communication media and its negative effects on the development of children and teenagers.

The "Bundesdrogenbeauftragte" (Federal Commissioner for Drugs) has commissioned the first extensive study on the health effects of modern media consumption in families conducted by German pediatricians.

According to the study, 600 000 teenagers are addicted to the internet and another 2.5 million young people are

in danger of becoming so. Moreover, even many preschool aged children use their parents' smartphones, often without supervision.

However, smartphone use can lead to health risks even in toddlers. There seems to be a link between parents' digital media use and feeding and sleeping disorders in infants. In children between 2 and 5 years of age there also seems to be a connection between their media habits and language as well as concentration problems.

F   Dealing with unknown words

a)   Guessing the meaning of unknown words when mediating from English to German (basic level)

English word or expression	Strategy used	Meaning
to document	other language (German: dokumen-tieren) word family (noun: document)	dokumentieren
preparation	word family (verb: to prepare) other language (German: präparieren)	Vorbereitung
unforgivable	prefix un- → negative meaning suffix -able → transforms a verb into an adjective	unverzeihlich
to come round	figurative meaning	to make a step towards the other; nachgeben, einlenken
dignified	word family (noun: dignity)	with dignity; würdevoll
commercial	other language (German: kommerziell)	kommerziell
justified	word family (noun: justice, adjective: just)	gerechtfertigt
entry	word family (verb: to enter) other language (French: entrer)	Eingang

b)   Paraphrasing unknown words when mediating from German to English (advanced level)

German word or expression	Strategy used	English word or expression
die Akzeptanz	other language (French: acceptance) word family (verb: to accept)	acceptance
sicherheitsbewusst	verbal phrase	concerned with / aware of safety
beispielhaft	synonym (German: exemplarisch)	exemplary
An- und Verkauf	prefix	buying and selling / purchase and sale
hoffnungsvoll	word parts: Hoffnung = hope, -voll = full	hopeful; full of hope
hinterlassen	word parts: hinter = behind; verlassen / zurücklassen = to leave	to leave behind
Angebot	other language (German: Offerte, French: offre) word family (verb: to offer)	offer
reservieren	synonym (German: buchen)	to book

G   Dealing with false friends

a)   Being aware of false friends (basic level)

What are false friends?

False friends are words or expressions that are often confused with a word in another language because they look or sound similar, but have different meanings. For example, the German noun "Handy" means "mobile phone", while in English the word "handy" is an adjective that means "convenient to handle or useful".

Why is it important to avoid false friends?

If you don't know about false friends, this can lead to severe misunderstandings between speakers of different languages. For example, the sentence "I can't find my handy" does not make any sense for English speakers who do not know about this false friend.

b) Recognizing false friends (basic level)

English word	German translation	False friend	English translation
actual	wirklich, tatsächlich, eigentlich	aktuell	topical, current, up-to-date
all day	den ganzen Tag	alle Tage	every day
also	auch	also	so
brand	Marke	Brand	fire
to become	werden	bekommen	to get, to receive
to blame sb.	jmd. verantwortlich machen	sich blamieren	to make a fool of yourself, to embarrass yourself
brave	tapfer	brav	good, well-behaved
brief	kurz	Brief	letter
chips	Pommes	Chips	crisps
consequent	folgend	konsequent	consistent
decent	ordentlich, annehmbar	dezent	discreet
dose	Dosis	Dose	tin (BE), can (AE)
engaged	verlobt	engagiert	dedicated, committed
eventual(ly)	schließlich	eventuell	maybe, perhaps
fabric	Stoff, Material	Fabrik	factory
fast	schnell	fast	almost
gift	Geschenk	Gift	poison
gymnasium	Turnhalle	Gymnasium	grammar school
handy	praktisch	Handy	mobile phone (BE), cell phone (AE)
meaning	Bedeutung	Meinung	opinion
murder	Mord	Mörder	murderer
must not	nicht dürfen	nicht müssen	to not need to
note	Notiz	Note	grade
to probe	prüfen	proben	to rehearse
prospect	Aussicht	Prospekt	brochure
Roman	römisch	Roman	novel
self-conscious	unsicher, befangen	selbstbewusst	self-assured
sensible	vernünftig	sensibel	sensitive
sympathetic	verständnisvoll	sympathisch	likeable

c) Avoiding false friends (advanced level)

1. Mein Chef ist tatsächlich annehmbarer, als ich gedacht hatte.
   Du darfst nicht zu verlegen sein.
   Ich verstehe nicht den Sinn dieses Geschenks.
   Der Plan, eine neue Turnhalle zu bauen, erschien ganz vernünftig.

2. He made a fool of himself with his opinion.
   Maybe I will receive an important letter tomorrow.
   The murderer actually seemed quite likeable.
   He lost his mobile phone in the fire.

H   Creating structure and coherence

a)   Expressions to create structure and coherence (basic level)

Getting started:	first (of all); firstly; to start with
Adding new ideas:	furthermore; moreover; on top of that; in addition (to that); secondly; the next point; after that; then; above all; in connection with; both … and …; either … or …; not … either; moving on
Giving reasons:	because; since; therefore; so that; in order to; as a result; consequently
Contradicting:	however; nevertheless; in contrast to; on the one hand …, on the other hand …
Conceding:	It is true that … but; although; even if; in spite of; whereas; while; even though
Concluding:	finally; eventually; last but not least; in the end; in conclusion; all in all; to conclude; to sum up; in short

b)   Using linking words and expressions to improve a given text (advanced level)

The "Bundesdrogenbeauftragte" (Federal Commissioner for Drugs) has commissioned the first extensive study on the health effects of modern media consumption in families conducted by German pediatricians.

According to the study, 600 000 teenagers are addicted to the internet **and another** 2.5 million young people are in danger of becoming so. **Moreover,** many pre-school aged children use their parents' smartphones, often even without supervision. **However,** smartphone use can lead to health risks, **even** for toddlers. There seems to be a link between parents' digital media use and feeding and sleeping disorders in infants. In children between 2 and 5 years of age there also seems to be a connection between their media habits and language as well as concentration problems.

2.2   Mediation practice

A   Ausbildungsplätze (Mediation German → English)

1.

German	English
Ausbildung	traineeship
arbeitslos	unemployed
Arbeitslosigkeit	unemployment
Jobsuche	job search
Bewerber/-in	job candidate
Arbeitsmarkt	labour market
Nachfrage	demand
Realschulabschluss	General Certificate of Secondary Education (GCSE)
Fachhochschulreife	advanced technical college entrance qualification
Abitur	A-levels
Schulabgänger/-in	graduate
Einzelhandel	retail
Bürokaufmann/-frau	office management assistant

2. Der Ausbildungsmarkt entwickelt sich zunehmend zu einem Bewerbermarkt. Das zeigen die jüngsten Daten der Bundesagentur für Arbeit. Demnach gab es 172 200 unbesetzte Ausbildungsplätze, aber nur 148 000 noch suchende Bewerberinnen und Bewerber. Das heißt, selbst wenn alle Bewerber eine Stelle finden, wären noch 24 200 Ausbildungsplätze unbesetzt. Noch nie waren zu Beginn des Ausbildungsjahres so viele Lehrstellen offen und noch nie war die rechnerische Lücke zwischen Nachfrage und Angebot so groß. Zum Vergleich: Im vergangenen

Jahr suchten 4,2 Prozent mehr junge Männer und Frauen noch einen Ausbildungsplatz – und 5,5 Prozent weniger offene Stellen. [...]

Das liegt zum einen an der zunehmenden Akademisierung: Immer weniger junge Erwachsene verlassen die Schule mit einem Realschulabschluss, viele Schulabgänger hängen noch ein paar Schuljahre bis zur Fachhochschulreife oder dem Abitur dran. Zum anderen rücken mit der sogenannten „Generation Z" die geburtenschwachen Jahrgänge in den Arbeitsmarkt nach. Außerdem bleibt auch die Berufswahl der Jugendlichen weitgehend tradi-

tionell. Die jungen Männer und Frauen wählen vor allem klassische Handel- und Kaufmannsberufe. Besonders im Handwerk fehlt der Nachwuchs. [...]

Laut Bundesagentur für Arbeit gehörten zu den zehn gefragtesten Ausbildungsberufen Ende Juli der Kaufmannsberuf mit Schwerpunkt Büromanagement, gefolgt von einer Ausbildung zum Einzelhandelskaufmann oder zur Einzelhandelskauffrau sowie einer klassischen Verkäufer-Ausbildung oder eine Ausbildung zum Industriekaufmann oder zur Industriekauffrau.

3.

Piece of information	Important? Reasons?
There are more vacancies than young people looking for a job or traineeship.	Relevant, key information of the article
There were 24 200 open training positions.	Too detailed; English teenagers do not need to know the exact numbers in a particular year
Last year, 4.2 % more young men and women were looking for a training position, while there were 5.5 % fewer vacant positions.	Too detailed; English teenagers do not need to know the exact percentages in a particular year
Currently there are more open training positions than ever.	Important; shows a trend
Young people mostly choose jobs in trade and business.	Important
The data on traineeships were published by the German "Bundesagentur für Arbeit."	Important where the data are from
Jobs in office management are more popular than jobs in retail.	Not relevant which jobs are more popular; the point of the article is which areas tend to be popular
The most popular traineeships are in office management, retail and trade.	Relevant: which areas are the most popular?

4. The article is about the increasing number of traineeship positions which cannot be filled, especially in skilled crafts and trades.

According to the "Bundesagentur für Arbeit" (Federal Employment Agency), the gap between available traineeship positions and demand is higher than ever. This is due to three factors. Firstly, more and more young people are choosing higher education rather than professional training. Secondly, the young people now entering the working world were born in years with low birth rates. Thirdly, young people mostly choose jobs in trade and business rather than in skilled crafts and trades. The most popular traineeships are in office management, retail and trade.

B Ein Ausflug nach Tschernobyl (Mediation: German → English)

1. Individual solutions

2.

German	English
Atomkraft	atomic energy
Atomkraftwerk	nuclear power plant
radioaktiv	radioactive
verstrahlt, verseucht	contaminated

German	English
Strahlung	radiation
Sperrzone, Sperrgebiet	restricted area
Beton	concrete
Atomreaktor	nuclear reactor
GAU (größter anzunehmender Unfall)	worst case scenario
Sarkopharg	sarkophargus
Geisterstadt	ghost town
Katastrophe	catastrophe

3.

	right	wrong	not in the text
The nuclear incident in Chernobyl took place in 1986.			×
Tourists can now go on guided bus tours to the restricted area around the former nuclear power plant.	×		
The bus tours to Chernobyl cost €100.		×	
The day trips to Chernobyl start in Kiev.	×		
The radiation around the former power plant is 10 times higher than as usual.		×	
Chernobyl is located in Ukraine, in the former Soviet Union.			×

4.

- Tagestour mit dem Bus von Kiew nach Tschernobyl bei Touristen sehr beliebt
- Kosten: 120 €, inklusive Führung und Sondergenehmigung für das Sperrgebiet
- Veranstalter übernimmt keine Verantwortung für mögliche Gesundheitsschäden
- bei der Tour wird die 30-Kilometer-Sperrzone rund um den ehemaligen Reaktor besucht, insbesondere:
  - stark verstrahlte ehemalige Dörfer, die nach der Katastrophe mit Erde zugeschüttet wurden
  - Wald in der Nähe des Reaktors, wo die Strahlung 1 000 Mal höher ist als am Reaktor selbst
  - Stop 300 Meter entfernt vom Sarkopharg um den ehemaligen Reaktor
  - verlassene Stadt, wo früher die Arbeiter des Kraftwerks gearbeitet haben, und Museum

5.

- day trip by bus from Kiev to Chernobyl as a tourist attraction
- costs: € 120, guided tour and special permit for the restricted area around the former nuclear power plant
- organizers of the tour do not take responsibility for potential health risks
- attractions on the tour:
  - highly irradiated villages near the reactor that were buried after the catastrophe
  - a forest near the reactor, where radiation is 1 000 times higher than at the reactor itself
  - a stop only 300 metres from the former reactor
  - a ghost city where the power plant workers used to live and the museum which is now located there

Transcript: „Ausflug nach Tschernobyl", Continuco / Cornelsen / ZDF Enterprises

Ausflug nach Tschernobyl, ein absoluter Renner bei Touristen. Die Tagestour von Kiew kostet 120 Euro, inklusive Führung und Sondergenehmigung fürs Sperrgebiet. Erster Stopp am Schlagbaum der 30-Kilometer-Zone rund ums Kraftwerk. Nach der Ausweiskontrolle muss jeder Teilnehmer unterschreiben, dass er die Veranstalter anschließend nicht wegen etwaiger Gesundheitsschäden verklagt. Das erste Mal Gänsehaut bei den Touristen.

„Ich hoffe, das ist nur Papierkram." – „Ich habe gerade ein bisschen komisches Gefühl."

Jurij, der Reiseführer der staatlichen Tschernobyl-Agentur weiß, was die Touristen sehen wollen. Er beginnt mit einem der begrabenen Dörfer, fünf Kilometer vom Reaktor entfernt. Hier war der radioaktive Niederschlag nach der Explosion besonders stark. Die Häuser wurden mit Bulldozern untergepflügt und sind bis heute unter Erdhügeln begraben. Verstrahltes Niemandsland.

Der Bus nähert sich der Reaktorruine. Die Spannung steigt. Plötzlich spielen die Geigerzähler verrückt. Wir sind im sogenannten Roten Wald. In diesem Waldstück gibt es Flecken, die stärker strahlen als der Sarkophag, erklärt Jurij und verbietet das Aussteigen. Von außen misst er die Radioaktivität für alle. Sie ist 1 000 Mal so hoch wie normal.

Und dann kommt der Moment, auf den alle gewartet haben. Der Stopp, 300 Meter vom Sarkophag entfernt. Ein paar Minuten, länger dürfen die Touristen nicht bleiben. Die Strahlung ist ungefähr 20 Mal so hoch wie normal. Die nach dem GAU eilig gebaute Betonhülle um den explodierten Reaktor wirkt brüchig und instabil.

Letzter Stopp der Tour ist Prypjat, Geisterstadt der Tschernobyl-Arbeiter. 50 000 Menschen haben hier einst gelebt. Hastig mussten sie ihr Zuhause für immer verlassen. Ein Museum der Sowjetunion und gleichzeitig der Ort, an dem die Katastrophe von Tschernobyl begehbar, begreifbar wird.

„Erdrückend. Bedrückend. Und ziemlich schwer zu verkraften.“

Der Touristentrip nach Tschernobyl geht zu Ende. Während der Bus am Rand der Sperrzone auf Radioaktivität untersucht wird, müssen die Passagiere durch die Strahlenmessgeräte. Das letzte Abenteuer des Trips. Weiß für sauber. Rot für verstrahlt. Alle dürfen gehen.

„Ich würde es jederzeit wieder machen, mit Leuten, die noch nie da waren. Ich würde es sehr empfehlen, wenn man sich damit auseinandersetzen will, zu sehen, wie das Ganze ist.“

So endet die Tagestour in die Sperrzone.

C Movie review: The Hunger Games (Mediation: English → German)

1. In a future version of North America a small, wealthy city rules over the rest of the impoverished nation. Every year, a number of the country's youngest inhabitants are randomly selected to fight to the death in The Hunger Games. This year, Katniss Everdeen (Jennifer Lawrence) will change the game.

   Probably the greatest achievement of The Hunger Games, and there are many, is that in adapting a phenomenally successful teen novel its creative team have produced something that works as a film, not just as an adaptation of a book. There's no required reading before entering the cinema in order to 'get it'. [...] The Hunger Games as a novel has been dissected, expanded and retooled into something intelligent, immersive and powerfully current. [...]

   Jennifer Lawrence is perfect as Katniss. There's very little softness about her, more a melancholy determination

that good must be done even if that requires bad things. [...]

The violence and cruelty is most explicit in the Hunger Games arena, a vast, synthetic forest where 24 children hunt each other, and the level of brutality is very smartly done. You don't get a rating suitable for a teenage audience by gutting preteens or decorating the landscape with their blood. So Ross cuts around it. The constantly searching, handheld camerawork used throughout the film comes in most useful during moments of violence, flashing round the action and making you think you've seen everything without ever really clocking anything that would upset your appetite. [...]

2. Worum geht es in dem Film?
   ● Zukünftige negative Vision des modernen Nordamerika.
   ● Eine kleine Stadt regiert über den Rest des verarmten Landes.
   ● Jedes Jahr werden einige Jugendliche zufällig ausgewählt, um in den sogenannten Hunger Games miteinander um Leben und Tod zu kämpfen.
   ● In diesem Jahr wird Katniss Everdeen die Hunger Games verändern.

   Wie ist die Verfilmung gelungen im Vergleich zur Romanvorlage?
   ● Der Film ist verständlich, auch wenn man das Buch nicht gelesen hat.
   ● Der Roman wurde verwandelt in einen intelligenten, eindringlichen und aktuellen Film.

   Was sagt der Rezensent über die Hauptdarstellerin?
   ● Sehr passend: Sie bringt Katniss' Härte und traurige Entschlossenheit sehr gut zur Geltung.

   Wie geht der Film mit Gewaltszenen um?
   ● Sehr gut: Die Gewalttätigkeit der Hunger Games wird deutlich, ohne das Gemetzelszenen direkt gezeigt werden.

D London Ghost Walks (Mediation: English → German)

1. If you want to encounter the darker recesses of haunted London, then be sure to join the only Ghost Walks to be led by Richard Jones – an *internationally renowned* authority on the ghosts of London who has written 22 books on the supernatural and who has been conducting walks around the Capital's most haunted places since 1982. [...]

   Richard is up to date on all the most recent paranormal happenings in London and he knows the places to take you to where ghosts are seen and supernatural activity is experienced.

In the course of these ghost walks, you'll enjoy a delightfully entertaining mix of thrills, chills, fun and fear as you make your way through atmospheric old byways where you will find yourself looking nervously over your shoulder, ever wary of who, or what, might be waiting around the next corner or lurking just a few graves along. [...]

2. Hi Christian,

es gibt Neuigkeiten zu unserem London-Trip: Ich habe gerade eine coole Sightseeing-Tour gefunden:

Dabei geht es durch die dunklen, unheimlichen und spukenden Ecken Londons. Die Touren werden geleitet von einem international anerkannten Experten für Geister in London, der schon diverse Bücher über das Thema geschrieben hat und die Geisterführungen durch London schon seit 1982 macht. Er kennt sich angeblich auch mit neueren paranormalen Phänomenen in London aus.

Bei der Führung werden stimmungsvolle alte Schleichwege und Orte besucht, an denen es spuken soll, und es werden Geschichten über Geister erzählt.

Die Führungen sollen gleichzeitig unheimlich, unterhaltsam und lustig sein.

Was meinst du, wollen wir das machen?

Gibt es schon Neuigkeiten wegen der Hotelbuchung?

Bin gespannt, von dir zu hören!

Bis bald, …

3 Test your competences

A Things to do in Australia (Mediation: English → German)

Obwohl Australien sehr groß ist, kann man die wichtigsten Sehenswürdigkeiten innerhalb von zwei Wochen sehen:
- Das Great Barrier Reef ist eine riesige Unterwasserlandschaft, wo man viele verschiedene Fisch-, Hai-, Wal-, Delfin- und Korallenarten sehen kann.
- An dem riesigen Gesteinblock Uluru mitten im Outback, der auch als Ayers Rock bekannt ist, und in der benachbarten Stadt Alice Springs im Zentrum Australiens kann man die Outback-Landschaft bewundern und viel über die Kultur der Aborigines, der australischen Ureinwohner, lernen.
- Die Great Ocean Road verbindet die Städte Melbourne und Adelaide im Süden Australiens und bietet wunderschöne Landschaften und Ausblicke mit Klippen, Surferstränden und Weinbergen.
- An der Westküste gibt es viele Naturschutzgebiete und wunderschöne Strände. Dort kann man viele große Tierarten wie Wale, Delphine, Rochen oder Meeresschildkröten beobachten.

E At the youth hostel (Mediation: English ↔ German)

1. Reservations and bookings: booking – to book; reservation – to make a reservation; room; reception; receptionist; bunk beds (Etagenbetten); single room; double room; twin room; bathroom; baggage (AE) / luggage (BE); check-in; to check in; to check out; to stay at a hostel; lift; lobby; room key; room number

What could possibly go wrong with a group reservation at a youth hostel:
No reservation made
Wrong reservation: too many rooms; not enough rooms; rooms too small; rooms without bathroom / bed linen; reservation without breakfast

2. You (in German, to your group's leader): Er sagt, dass für die Jungs nur zwei Vierbettzimmer gebucht wurden. Es ist also für einen unserer Jungs kein Bett da.
You (in English, to the receptionist): He is quite sure that he gave you the correct number of people when making the reservation. So how could this happen?
You (in German, to your group's leader): Es tut ihm sehr leid, es ist ihr Fehler. Der Empfangsmitarbeiter war selbst nicht da, als du die Reservierung gemacht hast, sondern sein neuer Kollege. Er schaut aber, was sich machen lässt.
You (in German, to your group's leader): Eine andere Gruppe hat heute Morgen abgesagt. Es sind jetzt drei Dreibettzimmer frei. Wollen wir dann die für die Jungs und die zwei Vierbettzimmer für die Mädchen nehmen?
You (in English, to the receptionist): Would that be more expensive?
You (in German, to your group's leader): Er sagt, da es ihr Fehler war, berechnen sie uns keine Extrakosten für den zusätzlichen Raum und die Dreibettzimmer.
You (in English, to the receptionist): Okay, we'll take the rooms. When can we go into the rooms?

B Parapark Frankfurt – Erlebnistest (Mediation: German → English)

1. Nachdem ich in Berlin schon so viele Live Escape Games testen durfte, hat es mich nach Frankfurt gezogen, denn da gibt es Parapark, das Urgestein unter den Live Escape Games in Deutschland. Ich habe mich schon lange auf den Besuch gefreut und nun war es endlich so weit.

Appartement 113 – Der Klassiker

Unser Team besteht heute aus 5 Leuten und wir haben natürlich vor, das Appartement 113 zu knacken. Der Raum ist dem ersten originalen Live Escape Game aus Budapest nachempfunden. Alle meine Teamkollegen haben noch nie zuvor ein Live Escape Game gespielt. Darum wird es umso spannender, was uns heute erwartet. Wir befinden uns in einem Hausflur wieder und neben uns sind zwei verschlossene Wohnungstüren. Eigentlich wollen wir so schnell wie möglich heraus, doch die Eingangstür ist ebenso fest verschlossen. Wir machen uns also auf die Suche nach dem Schlüssel nach draußen.

Das erste Rätsel ist sehr einfach zu lösen und schon befinden wir uns in einer der beiden Wohnungen. Hier suchen wir erst mal nach Hinweisen und Gegenständen, die uns weiterbringen sollen. Insgesamt gibt es viele verschiedene Rätsel und Aufgaben und einige habe ich schon mal vorher gesehen. Man sieht also, woher die anderen Anbieter teilweise ihre Ideen genommen haben. Dennoch ist der Raum knifflig und nur mit gutem Teamwork und ein paar hilfreichen Tipps von unserer Game Masterin schaffen wir es, das Appartement 113 zu lösen und am Ende wieder zu entkommen.

Die Deko der Räume ist recht schlicht, sodass man nicht überfordert ist. Der Fokus liegt hier klar auf den Rätseln. Trotzdem kann durch das Sounddesign und die typische Rätsel-Musik eine spannende Atmosphäre aufgebaut werden. Jetzt weiß ich, warum das Appartement als der Klassiker schlechthin gesehen wird.

Mein Team und ich hatten so viel Spaß, dass wir direkt noch den anderen Raum, das 9. Portal, ausprobieren wollen. [...]

2. Dear Laura,

Your visit is coming closer and I am already planning some fun activities for us. One of them, I think, will be Parapark Frankfurt. I have read an article by a young blogger who tested the game with some friends. According to the author Parapark Frankfurt is one of the oldest Live Escape Games in Germany. The classic game there is called "Apartment 113". The game is for small teams and also suitable for people who have never participated in a Live Escape Game.

The room is an imitation of the original Live Escape Game in Budapest. First you find yourself in a corridor with a front door and locked apartment doors. All the doors are locked and the aim is to get outside as quickly as possible.

So you have to solve riddles to find the key and get out. According to the author the first riddle is pretty simple and allows you to enter one of the apartments. Here participants have to look for clues and objects to help them find the next key. There are several different riddles and tasks, some of which are similar to those from other Live Escape Games. They are all pretty difficult, and so the tester and his team needed good teamwork and a few hints from the game master to solve the game and escape. According to the author, the decoration of the rooms is simple and not too overwhelming, with a focus on the riddles. The sound effects create an exciting atmosphere.

So, all in all, the tester and his team were positively impressed and are going to test the other apartment there as well.

What do you think? Would you like to go there?

I am already looking forward to seeing you!

Best wishes,

Your friend ...

C Boarding schools for international students (Mediation: English → German)

1. Choosing the right boarding school for your child can be a challenging experience. With countless institutions on offer worldwide, and varying fees from the manageable to the superstellar, increased cost doesn't always result in quality. Parents are bombarded with options, all while trying to find the ideal home-away-from-home which combines modern facilities with excellent pastoral care in a community environment. Increasingly, prestigious institutions around the globe are opening their doors to international students, offering excellent academic teaching with manageable fees.

Lasting friendships

Children and teenagers can enjoy an excellent education while experiencing a new culture and creating lifelong friendships. From sports to art and drama to music, students can form lasting friendships and familial-style bonds while learning a new skill or attribute. In fact, increasing numbers of parents are choosing a boarding school education for their children as it enables them to gain internationally recognized qualifications while learning how to build relationships with their peers during a child's important formative years.

International boarding schools are accustomed to the initial teething problems posed by homesickness and culture shock, meaning that each student is provided with specialized care and support during their first few weeks when everything feels new and friendships are established. [...]

Spreading their wings

Furthermore, a boarding school education will encourage students to become more independent, from managing their belongings, class timetable and even getting out of bed to make it to lessons, children soon become self-sufficient, driven individuals with excellent time management skills. [...]

Professional career focus

Choosing an international boarding school education for your child can help set them on a dynamic career path from a very young age. Boarding schools recognize and hone childrens' talents, supporting and encouraging them during their school life. Parents can be assured that boarding schools often possess links to world renowned universities and institutions. From Cambridge to Yale, choosing an international boarding school will continue to open doors within your child's educational and professional life.

Furthermore, international boarding schools offer activities which encourage students to learn and develop CV building skills alongside their full-time studies. Public speaking, debating society and even the chance to become a student prefect teach children responsibility and professional relationships, placing them at a distinct advantage in the student talent pool. Combining a traditional experience and high-calibre education ensures that international boarding schools produce well-rounded, talented individuals who stand out from the crowd. [...]

2. Argumente für einen Aufenthalt an einem Internat für internationale Schüler:
- viele angesehene Internate nehmen internationale Schüler auf
- hohes Bildungsniveau
- neue Kultur(en) kennenlernen
- neue, langfristige Freundschaften
- international anerkannte Abschlüsse und Qualifikationen
- breites Angebot an sportlichen und künstlerischen Aktivitäten
- Betreuer haben Erfahrung mit Problem beim Einleben und Heimweh und können individuell auf die Kinder eingehen
- man wird selbstständiger und lernt Zeitmanagement und Selbstorganisation
- Talente werden erkannt und gefördert

- internationale Internate können Kontakte zu hochklassigen Arbeitgebern und Universitäten vermitteln
- Fähigkeiten, die sich im Lebenslauf gut machen (z. B. vor Leuten reden, debattieren, soziales Engagement etc.), werden gefördert
- man lernt Verantwortungsbewusstsein und Professionalität

D On holiday in Brighton (Mediation: English ↔ German)

You (to your uncle, in German): Sie haben noch freie Räume. Wie lange wollen wir denn bleiben?

You (to the receptionist, in English): Three days, please.

You (to your uncle, in German): Welche Räume wollen wir nehmen? Sie haben Einzelzimmer, Doppelzimmer mit Doppelbetten und Doppelzimmer mit zwei getrennten Betten. Und alle Räume gibt es entweder mit eigenem Badezimmer oder mit Badezimmer im Gang.

You (to the receptionist, in English): How much are the rooms?

You (to your uncle, in German): Das Einzelzimmer kostet 45 Pfund, die Doppelzimmer 75 Pfund. Die Räume ohne eigenes Badezimmer kosten 30 Pfund für das Einzel- und 60 Pfund für das Doppelzimmer.

You (to the receptionist, in English): Is that with or without breakfast?

You (to your uncle, in German): Das kontinentale Frühstück ist im Preis inbegriffen, das englische Frühstück kostet nochmal 10 Pfund extra pro Person.

You (to the receptionist, in English): We'll just take the twin room with bathroom and the continental breakfast, please. Would it be possible to have a room with a sea view?

You (to your uncle, in German): Mit Meerblick gibt es nur noch Einzel- und Doppelzimmer mit Doppelbett.

You (to the receptionist, in English): Then we'll take a twin room without the sea view. Which floor is it? And is there a lift?

You (to your uncle, in German): Das Zimmer ist in der dritten Etage, und wir können den Aufzug da drüben benutzen. Und du müsstest bitte noch diese Formulare hier ausfüllen.